D0994733

GLOBE

TRAVEL GUIDE

SEYCHELLES

PAUL TINGAY

NEW
HOLLAND

GLOBETROTTER
TRAVEL GUIDE

First edition published in 1995 by
New Holland (Publishers) Ltd.
London • Cape Town • Sydney • Singapore

Copyright © 1995 in text: Paul Tingay
Copyright © 1995 in maps: Globetrotter
Travel Maps
Copyright © 1995 in photographs:
Individual photographers as credited.
Copyright © 1995 New Holland (Publishers) Ltd

ISBN 1 85368 419 8

New Holland (Publishers) Ltd
Chapel House, 24 Nutford Place, London W1H 6DQ

Editor: Donald Reid
Seychelles Consultant: Denise Johnson
Project Manager: Sean Fraser
Design Concept: Neville Poulter
Design and DTP: Lyndall Hamilton
Cartography: Globetrotter Travel Maps
Reproduction by Hirt & Carter (Pty) Ltd, Cape Town
Printed and bound in Hong Kong by South China Printing
Company (1988) Limited

Although every effort has been made to ensure accu-
racy of facts, and telephone and fax numbers in this
book, the publishers will not be held responsible for
changes that occur at the time of going to press.

Acknowledgements:
The publishers and author would like to thank Mick
and Kathy Mason; Alain and Ginette St Ange;
André, Linda and Roland Râssool; Marie-Anne
Hodoul; Raymond and Marie-Josée D'Espeville;
Georges and Margaret Norah; Loraine Pinder-
Browne; Marlene Pool.

Photographic credits:
Andrew Bannister, page 15; **Anthony Bannister**,
pages 61 (bottom), 80, 81, 96 (top) [ABPL]; **Kerstin
Beier**, pages 69 (top), 82 [ABPL]; **John Brazendale**,
Cover top right; **Camerapix**, pages 6, 8 (top), 8
(bottom), 13, 14, 19, 23, 25, 27, 28 (bottom), 29, 31
(top), 31 (bottom), 33, 35 (bottom), 41, 43, 44, 45, 49,
50 (top), 53, 56, 65 (bottom), 66, 67, 69 (bottom), 72,
76, 77, 84, 85, 88, 90, 92, 94, 99, 102, 106 (bottom), 107
(top), 107 (bottom), 108, 110 (bottom), 111, 112, 113,
114, 115 (bottom), 116 (top), 118, 119 (top), 120, 121;
Courtesy of *Fair Lady* **magazine (SA)**, Cover bottom
left, page 34; **Aaron Frankental**, Cover top left,
Cover bottom right, page 26 [ABPL]; **Peter
Lamberti**, Half-title, pages 12, 36, 38, 50 (bottom),
51, 75, 78 (bottom right); **Stefania Lamberti**, pages
10, 11, 59 (left), 59 (right), 83; **J. Mackinnon**, pages
28 (top), 119 (bottom); **Alan Mountain**, page 32;
Georges Norah (courtesy Paul Tingay), page 106
(top); **South African Library**, page 22; **Adrian
Skerrett**, pages 46, 62, 96 (bottom), 110 (top), 115
(top), 116 (bottom), 122 [CAMERAPIX]; **David
Steele**, pages 21, 30, 42, 64, 68, 78 (top) [PHOTO
ACCESS]; **Paul Tingay**, pages 16, 17, 18, 20, 47,
48, 61 (top), 65 (top), 91, 95, 98, 105, 109; **Patrick
Wagner**, pages 4, 35 (top), 60, 78 (bottom left), 79,
93 [PHOTO ACCESS]; **Duncan Willetts**, pages 52,
63 [CAMERAPIX].

CONTENTS

1
Introducing
Seychelles

The soaring mountains of Seychelles, covered with lush jungle, emerge from deep blue seas and a hundred glistening reefs. These Indian Ocean islands, 115 in all, stretch in a jewelled crescent from the equator to the tip of Madagascar. With a population of 75,000 Kreol-speaking inhabitants, whose ancestors came from Africa, India, and Europe, Seychelles was largely unknown until the construction of an airport 25 years ago introduced tourism to the islands.

Many of the islands are tiny palm-tufted coral specks where yours may be the only yacht to weigh anchor in a year. **Aldabra**, the world's largest atoll, and a World Heritage Site, is home to 150,000 giant tortoises. In the high mist forests of **Mahé** and **Silhouette** there are bats that eat mangoes, pitcher plants that gobble insects, and pygmy piping frogs the size of an emerald. The extraordinary beauty of the islands is such that nearly half of Seychelles landmass has been set aside as national park.

Mahé, the centre of Seychelles, is an island of sweeping beaches, secluded coves, and tin-roofed villages. Tales of buried pirate treasure abound and elegant plantation houses are tucked away under breadfruit trees. On neighbouring **Praslin** the presence of giant male and female coco de mer palms has given Seychelles its exotic reputation as the islands of love. The inter-island schooner calls at **La Digue**, where oxcarts trundle along the sandy roads. Some islands are strictly for the birds, others have a solitary, luxury lodge, while many seem to be no more than a mirage across the wide oceans.

TOP ATTRACTIONS

*** Beau Vallon Beach, Mahé: a classic sweep of sand, waves, and leaning coconut palms.
*** Morne Seychellois National Park: a mountainous living museum of exotic birds and plants.
** Vallée de Mai, Praslin: the home of the unique coco de mer forest.
** St Anne Marine National Park: exquisite fish and corals close to Mahé.
** Bird Island: millions of sea birds, emerald seas.
* La Digue: take the regular schooner ferry service from Praslin to the most traditional of the main islands.

Opposite: *The beach at Grand'Anse, on La Digue.*

- **World's largest tortoise**: there are 150,000 giant land tortoises on Aldabra. They weigh up to 150kg (330lb) and can stand a metre high.
- **Heaviest fruit**: the double nut of the coco de mer palm weighs 18kg (40lb), making it the heaviest fruit in the plant kingdom.
- **Rarest tree**: the jellyfish tree. Once thought to be extinct, there are no more than 50 in the world, all on Mahé's mountains.
- **Largest fish**: the world's largest fish, the whale shark, is a frequent visitor to the islands' coral reefs.
- **Wide-eyed bat**: the Seychelles fruit bat not only eats fruit, but it can see well.
- **Granite isles**: all other mid-oceanic islands in the world are formed by coral. The Inner Islands of Seychelles are the tips of continental granite mountains.

THE LAND

Millions of years ago, as fires burned and melted in the bowels of the earth, the supercontinent of Gondwana, which included much of the southern hemisphere, tore itself apart. India separated from Africa, the sea rushed in to fill gaping canyons, and deserts and plains were covered by fathomless ocean. It was a process that spanned aeons and embraced the genesis of countless new species of life on earth. Gradually the seasons settled to a gentler rhythm, and the continents assumed their familiar shapes. Left in the middle of the Indian Ocean after this awesome cataclysm were the tips of some of the highest mountains and a hundred isolated coral atolls, a necklace of pearls in a forgotten sea, islands that we now know as Seychelles.

The Granitic Islands

Scattered across some 400,000km² (154,000 sq miles) of sea in the western Indian Ocean, the islands of Seychelles are made up of two distinct geological types: coralline and granitic. Most mid-oceanic islands in the world are formed from coral and volcanic action; the exceptions are the Inner Islands of the Seychelles, which are the remnants of a continental granite landmass.

Mahé, the largest island, together with **Praslin**, **La Digue**, **Silhouette**, and the other granitic islands closest to it, account for nearly 50% of Seychelles' landmass. These are the islands where most Seychellois live, and where the majority of visitor facilities are located. They are all situated in a

Left: *Palm fronds peek out from among huge granite boulders. The ruggedness of the Inner Islands betrays their continental origins.*

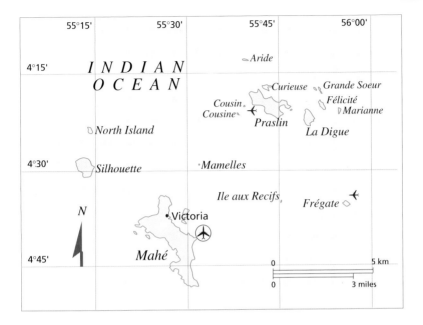

tight group in the northeastern part of the archipelago, 1600km (1000 miles) from Africa. Apart from towering black granite cliffs high in the mountains and the wavy, sculpted boulders that frame many deserted beaches, the granitic islands give the impression of being covered in impenetrable jungle. Mahé's mountainous Morne Seychellois National Park is a wilderness of tangled tropical splendour, but much of the greenery also comes from the profusion of coconut palms, wild cinnamon, and graceful albizia trees.

Mahé's beaches and coves are a continuous delight. They all have palms and gnarled takamaka trees shading them, the water is crystal clear and the swimming safe. A few hundred metres in front of most beaches are long lines of rumbling white water at the edge of the reef. The coastline is dotted with a series of tin-roofed villages each with its own church belltower, fishmarket and small guest houses.

40km (25 miles) east of Mahé and constantly visible as a blue ridge on the horizon, the second largest island, Praslin, hides the fabled coco de mer palm in its forested hills. La Digue, near Praslin, has one village, sandy roads, and unique pink-tinged granite boulders between an abundance of palms and delightful little coves. Silhouette, the third largest island, is to most people a mist-shrouded peak visible from Mahé's Beau Vallon Beach. A dozen other smaller granitic islands are dispersed around the larger ones, a number of them bird and nature sanctuaries.

The Coralline Islands

The 74 coral islands and atolls of Seychelles are the far-flung outposts of the group. They make up 47% of the land area of Seychelles, yet less than 500 of the islands' population of 75,000 live on them. During the last Ice Age the level of the Indian Ocean was much lower and there were thousands more, including now-submerged fishing banks.

Ile Denis and **Bird Island**, both coral islands, are normally grouped with the Inner Islands. The rest – tiny, horizon-floating islands tufted with palms – are called the Outer Islands, or *danzil* in Kreol, and are spread out like diamond dust across a vast expanse of ocean.

Many of them are only 3m (10ft) above sea level. Some islands have remote lagoons; all have wind-swept palms, talcum

Above: *An aerial view of Aldabra, one of the largest coral atolls in the world.*
Left: *Seychelles' delicate national flower, the tropic bird orchid.*

beaches and magical underwater gardens. **Aldabra** and **Farquhar**, the furthest from Mahé, each have a dozen islands, and the **Amirantes** group, named after the Portuguese explorer Admiral Vasco da Gama, twice that. Aldabra atoll, a ring of ferociously pitted limestone coral enclosing a lagoon 34km (21 miles) across, is a World Heritage Site and home to 150,000 giant tortoises, 2000 breeding turtles, and huge, tree-climbing crabs.

Ocean and Reef

The Indian Ocean dominates the Seychelles, whether by the immense depth of water just beyond the reefs, the influence of the oceanic weather patterns, or simply in the vast distances between the little specks of islands. Most visitors will come into contact with the ocean in some form or another: swimming in the warm, protected waters, or sailing on a schooner between the islands. Where meeting the ocean really becomes special, however, is under the water, diving and snorkelling on the edges of a vast new world of coral, waving polyps, fish, and overwhelming silence.

> **LIVING CORAL**
>
> All the coral islands of Seychelles were created from millions of skeletons of tiny animals called polyps.
> • Living polyps on the surface of the coral are attached to the limestone base of skeletons beneath them.
> • At meal times the polyps capture tiny plankton particles by swishing their sticky tentacles in the sea.
> • Coral prefers shallow water, and a sea temperature above 18°C (64°F).
> • Soft corals, leather corals and fan corals are the most beautiful. Other types are brain, stag and antler.
> • The collecting of coral in Seychelles is not allowed, but there are plenty of attractive (dead) pieces on the beaches.

After millions of years sitting in the ocean, even the granite islands have attracted a ring of coral around their shores. Coral atolls and islands are normally the result of coral growing around a geological formation, such as a volcano, which has sunk into the sea, leaving the crust of coral in place. Coral is a living thing, always growing, changing, and offering life to a vast chain of sea creatures, from minute plankton to the myriad of flashing fish, sharks and whales that find the waters of Seychelles so attractive.

At some points in the islands the reef is close enough to the shore for it to be exposed at low tide, which makes for a fascinating exploration, while along the beaches themselves there are always the scattered, delicate artistry of shells and dead coral.

Climate

Seychelles lies in the tropics between 4° and 10°S of the equator. The average **temperature** is 27°C (81°F), the average **humidity** a steamy 80%, and there are about seven hours of **sunshine** daily.

COMPARATIVE CLIMATE CHART	MAHE				PRASLIN				LA DIGUE			
	SUM JAN	AUT APR	WIN JULY	SPR OCT	SUM JAN	AUT APR	WIN JULY	SPR OCT	SUM JAN	AUT APR	WIN JULY	SPR OCT
AVE TEMP. °F	81	82	79	81	81	82	79	81	81	82	79	81
AVE TEMP. °C	27	28	26	27	27	28	26	27	27	28	26	27
SEA TEMP. °F	82	80	73	79	82	82	73	79	82	80	73	79
SEA TEMP. °C	28	27	23	26	28	28	23	26	28	27	23	26
HOURS SUN	5	8	8	8	5	7	8	8	5	8	8	8
RAINFALL in	16	7	3	4	12	5	4	6	12	6	3	8
RAINFALL mm	396	178	70	105	295	124	99	141	315	146	87	203

The refreshing southeast **trade winds** blow from April to October, when the weather tends to be cooler and drier, while the lighter northwest monsoon winds arrive during the Christmas period. At this time the **rain** can fall in torrential downpours, but there are short, showery spells any time of year. The force of the tropical showers means that the annual rainfall is 2300mm (90in), which is nearly four times that of London. However, being small islands in a wide ocean, Seychelles' many microclimates ensure conditions are very localized – it can be raining on one beach, sunny on the next, and misty up in the mountains.

The islands are at their windiest from April to September, which are the best sailing months. The coral islands are drier, warmer and, being at sea level, usually catch refreshing sea breezes. Only Farquhar atoll is within the normal cyclone belt.

Plant Life

The shoreline of the main granitic islands was once a jungle of almost impenetrable 30m (100ft) tall hardwood trees, but settlement, naval rivalry during the Napoleonic wars, and plantations soon devastated those. Even today, however, the impression is still of a dominating botanic riot of dense breadfruit trees, flame trees, and banyans. Old coconut and cinnamon plantations are everywhere,

Right: *A cluster of coco de mer nuts on a female palm.*

and wild fruits grow in every backyard: mangoes,
bananas, tamarinds, star-shaped *karambol*, fluffy fruited
prunes de France, and prickly *frizite*. Alongside the requis-
ite palms on every beach there are shading takamaka and
casuarina trees, whose tiny cones create a minefield for
barefooted bathers. Among the 75 tree and plant species
unique to Seychelles are the wild *bilenbi*, whose tart fruit
actually grows on the trunk of the tree, and possibly the
rarest tree on earth, the *bwa mediz*. Lost to botanists since
1908, its rediscovery 60 years later caused quite a stir at
Kew Gardens in London. There are only about 50 in the
world, all in the high mountains of Mahé. It is a bushy,
rather unspectacular tree, which takes its name, jellyfish
tree, from its umbrella-shaped fruit.

Lording over the botanical castle, however, is the
giant **coco de mer** coconut palm, whose male catkins
and double female nuts bear a striking resemblance to
the respective human reproductive organs. The Vallée
de Mai nature reserve on Praslin Island is the last natural
preserve of these monster palms which are endemic to
(i.e. they originate uniquely from) Seychelles. The shapely
nut is the largest fruit in the plant kingdom, and has been
the focus of much legend and mystery over the years.

> ### LULU THE GHOST CRAB
>
> *Trouloulou*, in Kreol, the
> ghost crab, is the mischievous
> thief of the sands. It preys on
> hatchling turtles and is in
> turn preyed upon by fisher-
> men who use these delicate
> sand dancers as bait. Lulu is
> hilarious to watch, particular-
> ly at night, peak revelry time,
> as she skitters in jerkstart six-
> by-six sprints across a pristine
> moonlit beach. Frightened,
> she will hunker down pre-
> tending to be invisible, then
> rush on tiny tiptoes for bur-
> row or surf.

Below: *The graceful fairy
tern, with its unusual dark
blue and black beak.*

Creatures of Land, Sea and Air

Seychelles may once have
been linked to Africa but it
has none of that contin-
ent's big game. Rat, hare,
hedgehog-like tenrec,
dogs, and even some wild
goats (on Aldabra) are the
only terrestrial mammals
in residence, all of which
have been introduced. The
only endemic mammals
are bats, among them the
giant fruit bat, which
unlike other bats, can see.

Giant land tortoises are only found in two places in the world: the Galapagos islands off South America, and Seychelles. They grow up to 1m (3ft) high, weigh 150kg (330lb) and at least some are believed to be 200 years old. There are four types of frog on the islands, which have noisy concerts in the Mahé mountains. The female tree frog grows to 20cm (8in), somewhat overshadowing her spouse, who measures a mere 5cm (2in). After the early extermination of the Nile crocodiles, the only other land reptiles are geckos and skinks. The bright emerald green gecko will shed its wriggling tail as a ruse to distract an advancing predator.

There are 3500 insect species in Seychelles, most unique to the islands, including Frégate Island's giant tenebrionid beetle, and the Seychelles leaf insect, whose camouflage drag far out-classes the African variety.

Millions of birds migrate from as far as the Arctic circle to the coral islands of Seychelles to breed. Some of the islands, such as Aride and Cousin, host some spectacular and noisy colonies of sea bird, including noddies, terns, and frigate birds. A number of varieties are unique to

Right: *A giant tortoise, often confused with and closely related to the turtle, (opposite). Both are found in Seychelles. The turtle has a flatter shell, and its legs have developed into paddle-like flippers.*

Seychelles, and are constantly under threat of extinction. Amongst these are the Seychelles kestrel, blue pigeon, bulbul, the beautiful black paradise flycatcher, and the whistling black parrot, which flies amongst the coco de mer trees on Praslin and is the national bird of Seychelles.

Sea Life

Dolphins, whales and manta rays are all common in Seychelles waters. The dugong or seacow was once here too and is remembered in the original name for Bird Island, Ile aux Vaches (Isle of Cows). The larger sharks usually stay in deep waters, although the plankton-feeding whale shark, the largest fish in the world, is sometimes encountered by divers. The marine turtle nests on a number of the islands, though nowadays all four species in Seychelles – green, hawksbill, loggerhead, and the giant leatherback – are all under threat from that relentless predator, man. Fighting fish such as marlin and tuna are also found and caught around the islands. Perhaps the most beautiful is the sailfish, which will leap out of the water shivering its silvery blue body in the sun.

Along the coral reefs there are a thousand flashing, darting and amazingly colourful reef fish. In the underwater forest you will see angelfish, parrotfish, cave-defending moray eels, hovering trumpetfish and the occasional turtle winging away in fright. There are black spiky sea urchins, tiger cowries, half-metre long crayfish and, occasionally, the protected *triton* conch shell blown by fishermen in early days to announce fish for sale.

DEVIL OF THE DEEP

The plankton-eating manta ray, or *diable de mer*, does not deserve its demonic name, for you cannot find a more graceful and harmless creature in the warm tropic waters. They look like huge smooth bats, their pectoral wings spanning up to 7m (23ft), often in flights of six or more. They can weigh as much as 1300kg (2900lb). Seychelles fishermen will harpoon them from small boats, but the manta is powerful and will easily drag a boat. Their devil-fish tag comes from the hornlike fins on either side of its head. In the days of slavery, plantation owners were fond of whips made from manta tail.

DOOMED TURTLES

Not long ago turtles from the outer islands would be stacked like boxes on the decks of ships, and, crying and sighing all the while, transported to the Long Pier pool on Mahé to be slaughtered for steaks, salted *kitouz*, and the calipee (fat) used in Europe to make turtle soup. Their yellow pingpong ball eggs were also stolen to make cakes. They have survived for over 100 million years yet now are threatened with extinction. In times past 6000 green turtles were caught annually in Cosmoledo. Today in neighbouring Aldabra there are only 2000 breeding females left. Fortunately they are slowly increasing in numbers, but turtles are still hunted in Seychelles, proof that more still needs to be done by a caring government, if time is not to turn turtle on these gentle creatures.

Conserve with Care

Although 46% of Seychelles land area is protected in one form or another, it often seems as if the whole of Seychelles is one large and extraordinarily beautiful park: island and beach, mountain and forest, reef and ocean.

The 18ha (45 acres) **Val de Mai** on Praslin, the home of the coco de mer palms, is one of Seychelles' two World Heritage Sites. The other is the 34km (21 mile) long **Aldabra** atoll, with its giant tortoises, rare birds and green turtle breeding grounds. Tiny **Cousin Island** near Praslin comes under the umbrella of the International Council for Bird Preservation, while not too far away on La Digue Island the small **La Veuve Reserve** is trying to conserve and nurture the last few pairs of long-tailed Seychelles black paradise flycatcher, one of the most threatened birds in the world.

Sea birds may not be disturbed on nine designated islands, spear fishing is prohibited everywhere, and the collecting of coral and shells, as well as fishing, is prohibited in the marine national parks. Tortoiseshell, corals and large shells are, however, still sold at curio stalls.

On some of the islands where the tree populations were devastated by plantations, reforestation schemes have been introduced. A number of transplantation schemes are being attempted for trees, birds, and even

Right: *The green sparkling undergrowth of the Vallée de Mai, one of Seychelles two protected World Heritage Sites.*

tortoises. And although it does have its economic rationality as well, the ceiling placed by the Seychelles government on the number of hotel beds will go a long way to prevent the destruction of the islands' unique ecosystem at the altar of tourism.

HISTORY IN BRIEF

The Indian Ocean is recognised as the birthplace of long distance sailing, with ancient Egyptian, Indian and Chinese texts indicating that there was sea-borne trade between India and Africa as long ago as 2000BC. Polynesians setting out from the Bay of Bengal on their great canoes sailed both east into the Pacific and west to the Maldives and Madagascar. The Phoenicians are known to have rounded the southern tip of Africa and Indian sailors commissioned by the kings of Gujerat in the 6th century were colonising Java, Bali and Madagascar. It is more than likely that some of these intrepid sailors stumbled upon the tiny mid-oceanic islands of the Seychelles on their voyages, perhaps taking a little time to explore them, catch a tortoise that offered some longed-for fresh meat, and perhaps plant a few crops to sustain them, before disappearing on their way again over the blue horizon.

Above: *An ageless Arabic dhow, still a common sight in many different parts of the Indian Ocean.*

Dhows in the Sea of Zanj

The first true records of the Seychelles date from AD851, a time when Arab merchant seamen from the Persian Gulf in their lateen-rigged dhows made good use of the January monsoon winds blowing from India towards Africa, and then the opposite southeasterly trades a few months later, to navigate the ocean they called the Sea of Zanj, or Sea of Blacks.

In AD916, the geographer Abu Zaid al Hassan referred to the 'high islands beyond the Maldives', which is generally considered to be a reference to the uniquely mountainous Seychelles. The Arabs called the granitic Inner Islands of the Seychelles 'Zarin', or Sisters – a possible reference to the seven sisters of the Pleiades constellation – and as they are known to have brought

---

THE ROC

Arab sailors believed the Seychelles to be the islands of the mythological *rukh*, or giant roc bird. The legends said that the coco de mer tree grew up from beneath the ocean (hence its name – coco de mer, or coconut of the sea), and its branches provided a roosting place for the mighty bird with its 45m (150ft) wingspan which could carry off elephants, and would surely do the same to any sailor who came too close. Marco Polo recounted this tale to Kubla Khan in China 700 years ago, who immediately dispatched an envoy with instructions to return with a quill from the fabulous bird.

the first coconut palm from India to the East African coast they may well have introduced it to Seychelles too. It is also clear that the coco de mer (which is endemic to Seychelles) was valued by Indian and Maldivan princes. At Anse Lascars on Silhouette and on Frégate Island there are Arab graves and ruins of coral brick buildings.

Portuguese Pioneers

500 years ago, fired by the missionary zeal of **Prince Henry the Navigator**, the tiny caravels of Portugal under the command of **Vasco da Gama** braved storms and scurvy to journey around the Cape of Good Hope towards India and Japan. The Amirantes Islands of the Seychelles or 'Isles of the Admiral', were named in 1502 in honour of Da Gama's promotion to the rank, but these first Europeans were not to settle on any of the islands they encountered. Within a few years the Portuguese had destroyed the Arab trade stranglehold on the Indian Ocean, and Portuguese names now dot the Indian Ocean: Chagos, Comoros, Rodrigues, Agalega, Diego Garcia and Cosmoledo, an atoll to the east of Aldabra.

Surveys, Spices, and Settlements

The first Englishmen to visit the islands that were to become their colony did so in 1609, with diarist **John Jourdain** giving us the first detailed picture of Seychelles. A hundred years later English and American pirates harried out of the Caribbean turned their swashbuckling attentions from the Spanish Main to the trade of spices, silks, tea, and timber that was crisscrossing the Indian Ocean. Famous buccaneers such as **Captain Kidd**, **'Long John' Avery**, **George Taylor**, and hook-nosed **Olivier le**

BOILED TORTOISE, MISTER MIDSHIPMAN

The English East Indiaman, the *Ascension*, anchored in Seychelles for 10 days in 1609. John Jourdain, one of the crew, wrote the first known account of the islands: 'About nine in the morninge we descryed heigh land', that had '... noe signe of any people that ever had bene there'. In this 'earthly paradise' they were 'allagartes' and (according to another observer, William Revett) '... many trees of 60 and 70 feete without sprigge except at the topp ... shipp tymber as the lyke or better cannot bee seene'. The crew availed themselves of the '... many coker nutts, both ripe and greene ... and much birde and fowle and tortells', which the crew, hungry for meat after so long at sea, fell upon, but after a few meals rejected because '... they did looke soe uglie before they were boyled'.

Vasseur (known as *La Buse*, the Buzzard) roamed the lucrative seas, and found the deserted coves of Seychelles ideal places to hide, careen ships and bury plunder.

A rusty old anchor at Anse Boileau beach on Mahé marks the spot where French Captain **Lazare Picault** landed in 1742 to survey the Seychelles for Governor Mahé de Labourdonnais of Mauritius. He gave the island the name Ile d'Abondance, and only later Mahé, in honour of his superior. 14 years were to pass before Commander **Corneille Nicholas Morphey** (of Irish-French descent) laid the official Stone of Possession on the shore of Victoria harbour, and – astutely for an aspiring naval officer – renamed the group of islands Séchelles after the French finance minister .

The French authorities in Ile de France (Mauritius), nervous of British colonial ambitions, were keen to back up their claim with actual occupancy, and so in 1770, encouraged by **Pierre Poivre**, an administrator of Ile de France who thought Seychelles could rival the Dutch East Indies in the cultivation of spices, the first group of settlers and slaves landed on St Anne's Island.

A small 'Etablissement', or capital, was built on Mahé, but the settlers grew few spices, and the colony survived rather than prospered.

The treasure of buccaneer Olivier le Vasseur is the most famous of the riches supposedly buried around the islands. The search has concentrated around Bel Ombre beach on Mahé, yet neither there, nor on any of the other islands around Seychelles where tantalising tales of treasure abound, has anything beyond a few silver coins and a pistol or two ever been found. Or if there has, no-one is telling. Still, there is a Pirates Bay, a 'corsair' restaurant, a murdered buccaneer's tombstone in the National Museum, and a Pirates Arms hotel. Roman Polanski filmed 'Il Pirato' in Seychelles. And what with a little yo ho ho and a bottle of local *bacca* rum, it all makes sound tourism sense.

Opposite: *A rusting anchor at Anse Boileau on Mahé serves as a monument to the landing of the first French surveying expedition of 1742, led by Lazare Picault.*
Left: *The lure of Seychelles from the time of the first settlers: coconuts, spices, and a marquetry box made from some of the valuable local hardwoods.*

THE CAPITULATIONS

Jean-Baptiste Queau de Quinssy, Governor of Seychelles during the Napoleonic Wars, was a master at changing sides. Seven times he capitulated to British warships entering Victoria harbour, each time welcoming French ships as soon as the enemy's back was turned. As his superiors in Mauritius fumed, his wily leadership and quick tongue allowed his tiny colony to flourish, albeit with continuous alarums as to which flag should be flying when a ship was spotted approaching. In 1804, after a few close shaves, De Quinssy managed to persuade the British of the reality of his position, and won a concession that allowed Seychellois vessels to ply the oceans unmolested under a neutral blue flag inscribed 'Seychelles Capitulation'. De Quinssy is buried at Government House, not far from the site of the flag pole he masterfully manipulated so many times.

Cannonballs and Capitulations

The French Revolution in 1789 set off a series of reactions around Europe that led to 20 years of war and the rise and fall of Napoleon. By 1794, when a new Commandant, **Chevalier Jean-Baptiste Queau de Quinssy**, arrived in the islands, Britain and France were at war, and the Indian Ocean was of growing strategic importance. The Seychelles were still in theory ruled from Mauritius, but they were remote and vulnerable.

On 16 May 1794, a squally day, when the island had been awake for a mere two hours, Commodore **Henry Newcome** of the British Royal Navy entered Victoria harbour, rather unsportingly flying a French flag. Faced by a combined British squadron firepower of 166 cannon and 12,500 trained men, De Quinssy remonstrated for honours sake and then surrendered.

Down came the tricolor, up went the Union Jack to a gentlemanly roll of drums and presentation of arms. Two weeks later the British sailed off, and the tricolor was back at the top of the flagpole with the *au revoirs* still ringing in the air. With alternate visits from French and British men o'war, De Quinssy became rather adept at welcoming first one side, then the other, supplying both with food, water, and a berth for repairs, while all the time acting as a refuge for French corsairs such as the notorious and dashing **Jean François Hodoul**.

Britain captured Mauritius in 1810, which still theoretically included the Seychelles, but their only concern for the islands was that the enemy did not use them. The mercurial De Quinssy, showing typical political astuteness, anglicized his name to suit his new rulers, became De Quincy, and carried on as Chief Justice on Mahé until his death in 1827.

Right: *Jean François Hodoul, or Le Corsair, renowned gentleman pirate.*
Opposite: *A typically overgrown plantation scene on Praslin.*

The Colonial Backwater

At this stage cotton, manioc, and a dozen different spices were being grown by a population of 1800, of whom all but 300 were slaves. 1835 saw the abolition of slavery and Seychelles was obliged to change from field husbandry to a total plantation economy (with crops such as coconuts, cinnamon, patchouli and vanilla), which did not require a large labour force. Former slaves were not interested in working on the plantations where, as they put it, 'the money is good, but too expensive'. The British adopted a policy of landing freed slaves on Seychelles (a total of 2500 over the years) where they were soon hired as labourers under 'apprenticeships', though with stinted rations, inadequate wages and rough treatment, their lives were hardly improved.

Saddled with a poor colony she did not want, Britain allowed Seychelles, for the rest of the 19th century and a good part of the next, to remain a peaceful, rather old-fashioned backwater visited by the occasional steamer and eccentric Victorian traveller. Among these were Marianne North, a botanist painter, and General 'Chinese' Gordon, who developed his eccentric theory of the biblical Genesis among the mysterious coco de mer palms of Praslin Island.

It was during the 19th century of splendid isolation and benign British *laissez faire* that the culture of Seychelles was formed – a mix of master and slave, planter and fisherman, France and Africa. Various crops and industries came and went over the years, including vanilla, copra, cinnamon, guano, and even whaling, but none seemed to last for long. The French farmers disliked their

---

SLAVERY

The first 15 settlers in 1770 on St Anne's Island included seven slaves, and the economy of the islands was to depend on this cheap labour for the next 70 years. Slavery in the Seychelles was reasonably benevolent and not perhaps as harsh as in other parts of the world, but a person enslaved in the islands still suffered the threat of iron halter, chain and manta ray whip, along with appaling restrictions on movement, possessions, housing, marriage and the right to their children. Worst of all, perhaps, was the memory of abduction and the obliteration of cultural roots. To this day in Seychelles many appear reluctant to marry and the music of the islands, *moutia*, seems at times to reflect an indefinable loss and need for relationship and certainty.

BORN TO BE KING

In 1805 one Pierre Louis Poiret arrived in Seychelles. He always maintained (as did 40 others) that he was the legitimate heir to the French throne, son of Marie Antoinette and Louis XVI, and that he had been smuggled out of the Temple Prison in Paris and given as a child to a cobbler, whose name, Poiret, he took. Always deferred to with royal respect, he farmed on both Poivre and Mahé Islands and died at the age of 70 in 1856. Although never formally married, he left seven children, all of whom were named, in royal fashion, Louis or Louise.

British rulers and in turn the British were disdainful. With the arrival in 1850 of the first Indian merchants, and in 1895 a few Chinese, the Kreol kaleidoscope of the islands was complete.

The 20th Century

Seychelles eased gradually into the 20th century. In 1903 she emerged from under the skirts of Mauritius to take up status as a fully-fledged colony. To mark this momentous development a Clock Tower was erected in the middle of Victoria, and for nearly 100 years it has been the centre of town and focus of traffic, business and sophistication. In the islands, if you had not seen the *horloge* you were considered a country hick.

During these years Indian indentured labourers built a road over the mountains to every visitor's favourite beach, Beau Vallon; Catholic churches and two secondary schools were established, and the British administration strived mightily and unsuccessfully to anglicize language and culture. The lovely iron-filigreed hospital near the Botanical Gardens was built: with elephantiasis, amoebic dysentery, and leprosy it was much needed. The first car arrived, and in 1926 electricity hesitantly arrived to light the centre of town.

During World War II several contingents of Seychelles soldiers fought in the desert campaign. For many Seychellois it was the first taste of equality and freedom. Some stayed on in the British army, providing Rs650,000 in wages annually to 3000 poorer families. Their return in the early 1950s was a financial setback, but it was the source of much excitement. 'Maman, the Tobruks have come back', the folksong went, 'what an occasion, Maman, I'll die or go mad, if I don't find a husband'.

Below: *The Victoria Clock Tower, not long after it was erected to commemorate the granting of full colonial status to Seychelles in 1903.*

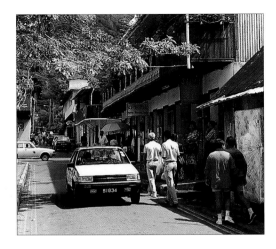

Left: Ornate balconies and corrugated iron roofs imbue Market Street in Victoria with a casual, timeless quality.

Immediately after the war **Dr Percy Selwyn-Clarke**, medical officer in the notorious Japanese POW camp at Stanley in Hong Kong, became the first Governor appointed by a socialist government in London. 'I will have no colour bar in this colony' he declared, thus disenfranchising himself immediately in the esteem of the chattering classes down at the club, though his period as governor is kindly remembered by the Seychellois.

A Tale of Two Lawyers

And it was time for politics. A taxpayers association was formed and in 1940 the colonial legislative council permitted four elected members. In 1964, two political parties were formed: the Democratic Party, led by ebullient lawyer **James Mancham** (whose family ran a popular supermarket, Richards', in Victoria), and the broader-based Seychelles Peoples United Party, also led by a lawyer, **Albert René**. 30 turbulent years on, these two men remain at the centre of the country's political stage.

Universal adult suffrage arrived in 1967, but the great leap forward for Seychelles was to opt for tourism as the mainstay of the islands' economy. When the airport was constructed in 1971, the landing of the first VC10 was watched by practically the whole island.

EXILES IN EDEN

After an assassination attempt, Napoleon decided to banish 76 Jacobin 'terrorists' to Seychelles. The practice was to become quite established. Among the more prominent exiles were:

● 1877 **Sultan Abdullah of Perak**, whose successor spent his boyhood on Mahé and composed a song which for a while became the islands' national anthem.

● 1900 **King Prempeh II of Ashanti West Africa**, who arrived dressed in leopard skins, accompanied by his favourite executioner.

● 1916 **Seyyid Khalid bin Barghash of Zanzibar**, sent to Seychelles for being friendly to the Kaiser.

● In 1922 Winston Churchill toyed with the idea of of sending 500 **Irish political prisoners** to Praslin.

● 1937 Members of the **Arab Higher Committee** who refused to accept the partition of Palestine.

● 1956 **Archbishop Makarios of Cyprus**; he stayed a year, was reputed to sing well, and enjoyed his Cypriot wine.

Five years later, on 29 June 1976, Seychelles became independent from Britain and the bearded and Saville Row–besuited Mancham took over from the cockaded governor. Henceforth two portraits adorned public buildings in Seychelles: one of the incumbent, President Mancham, and the other, with a leaner, somewhat

Above: *Albert René (left), the current president, and James Mancham (right), the leader of the opposition, meet a British government minister at a constitutional conference in 1976.*

hungrier look, of Prime Minister René.

The following year, while Mancham was at a Commonwealth Conference in London, Réne pounced with a coup d'état. With Tanzanian troops standing by in Dar es Salaam as a back up, his men took the broadcasting centre, the police station and power. Two men were killed, one – an insurgent – became a hero while the other – a policeman – did not. Guns appeared in the streets, a curfew was announced, arrests were made and a peoples' militia formed. The revolution for *liberté, égalité, fraternité* had taken place, but as René was the people's choice anyway, history may well decide that it was unnecessary.

HISTORICAL CALENDAR

250 million years ago, the supercontinent of Gondwana splits up, leaving a few islands in the Indian Ocean. Among them, Seychelles.
2000BC – AD500 Chinese, Egyptian, Indian, Greek, Roman, and Phoenician explorations of the Indian Ocean. Some probably visited Seychelles.
AD851 First Arab recorded sighting of Seychelles.
AD1275 Marco Polo tells Kublai Khan of the (mythological) 'roc' bird in the Indian Ocean.

1502 Amirantes islands named after Admiral Vasco da Gama, Portuguese navigator.
1609 First British landing. Recorded by John Jourdain.
1742 First French landing by Lazare Picault.
1756 Stone of Possession laid on Mahé. Islands named Séchelles; first settlement follows in 1770.
1794 Napoleonic era. Commandant de Quinssy capitulates for the first of seven times to British warships arriving in Seychelles.

1814 Seychelles ceded to Britain.
1835 Abolition of slavery.
1903 Seychelles becomes a colony in its own right.
1971 Airport opened by Queen Elizabeth; tourism soars.
29 June 1976 Independence from Britain. James Mancham becomes President.
5 June 1977 Prime Minister Albert René seizes full power in coup d'etat.
1993 First multiparty elections won by René. Mancham is leader of opposition.

The Modern Era

Changes came quickly in the next two decades. It was, for the Seychellois, the best of times and the worst of times. Tourism soared, the economy boomed, construction flourished. New schools, old age homes, and health facilities all arrived. A confident spirit of nationhood fired *le peuple,* who soon became well nourished, well clothed, educated and employed. But it was also a time of counter-coups, plots and fear. In 1981 a group of South African mercenaries, led by 'Mad' Mike Hoare and joined by out-of-work Rhodesian Selous Scouts, launched an abortive invasion masquerading as a visiting rugby team. They were stopped at the airport and later, in quixotic Seychelles fashion, pardoned. In a bid to end the constant paranoia about invasions and intrigue, René stepped up his rhetoric against the exiled 'Movement for the Resistance', which was dealt a mortal blow in 1985 when its talented young leader Gerard Hoarau fell to a mysterious assassin's bullet in a London street.

Political instability is never good for tourism, and as the numbers of holidaymakers began to yo-yo, so the economy started to sour, the Mafia crept in, and many of René's disillusioned lieutenants abandoned their leader. The Catholic church intensified its criticism, and pressure at home and abroad mounted for a return to free elections. Wily as ever (touched, perhaps, by De Quincy's spirit?) René suddenly reversed direction and agreed to an election in 1993, only to knock the wind out of everyone's sails by winning 60% of the vote, and so retaining the Presidency.

Opposition was at least now legal, journalistic criticism allowed, and Mancham was back in Seychelles after 17 years, in parliament as leader of the opposition Democratic Party. After so many years of internecine squabbling, the two very different lawyers, both genuine patriots, opted for reconciliation.

Below: *One of Air Seychelles' inter-island fleet. The airline is one of the symbols of both the nation's embrace of the modern commercial world, and the effective promotion of the islands as an exclusive holiday destination.*

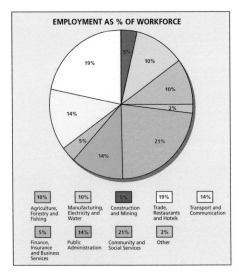

EMPLOYMENT AS % OF WORKFORCE

10%	10%	5%	19%	14%
Agriculture, Forestry and Fishing	Manufacturing, Electricity and Water	Construction and Mining	Trade, Restaurants and Hotels	Transport and Communication

5%	14%	21%	2%
Finance, Insurance and Business Services	Public Administration	Community and Social Services	Other

GOVERNMENT AND ECONOMY

The democratic multiparty elections of 1993 were a major step for Seychelles, and it will probably always be a democracy now. A republic within the Commonwealth, and a member of the Organisation of African Unity (OAU), the growth of the economy and encouraging signs of reconciliation have given Seychelles a more respected voice in international affairs. Yet the islands are small, tend to be politically claustrophobic, and they do have a lingering attachment to a centrally-controlled economy and one-party government.

Economy

For most of its inhabited life, the economy of Seychelles meandered along based on **fishing** and a few fluctuating **crops**, but nowadays, thanks to **tourism**, it has far greater potential. Although Seychelles does have a substantial balance of trade deficit, this is to a large part balanced by tourism receipts. France is by far the largest trading partner, with the United Kingdom next.

Seychelles boasts a *per capita* income on a par with many western countries, and certainly well above that of her African neighbours. Poverty is unknown, and with a minimum wage and old age pension there is a reasonably fair distribution of wealth. While infant mortality 30 years ago was as high as 58%, today it is 12%, and the birth rate has halved. Literacy is high, and Seychelles, democratic and dynamic, is beginning to show that it is a nation with both the human resources and the imagination to continue the encouraging forward momentum. In particular, the more relaxed political and economic climate is attracting young Seychellois back to the islands.

ECOTOURISM

The impressive record of Seychelles in conservation is reaping benefits as the holiday industry orientates itself towards ecotourism. Destinations around the world where tourism, the natural environment, and the local population work together are being increasingly promoted, and with 20% of the workforce employed directly in tourism, and many more benefiting through related spin-offs, Seychelles responds well to such demands. Where the islands also score is in the breadth of their appeal – to bird-watchers, botanists, divers, sailors, historians, walkers, and, as is the case for the majority, those who simply want to relax on some of the most beautiful beaches in the world.

A Holiday Package

Once upon a time the British Indian Steam Navigation liners would call monthly in Seychelles, and the occasional British warship would appear, show a film on Gordon Square (now Freedom Square) and play a football match against the local team. Until the airport was built in 1971 the Seychelles were the forgotten islands.

Above: *The Equator Sun Hotel on Mahé. The number of hotel beds is strictly monitored in Seychelles, in a bid to avoid the worse excesses of tourism.*

While the coming of tourism has exposed the somewhat shy Seychellois to prying cameras, consumer brand-names, topless bathers and foreigners tramping through their garden, the money is good and with few natural resources other than its beauty and its people, it was always going to be the one industry that Seychelles could exploit on any realistic economic scale. Apart from the jitteriness of an ever-fickle market (for example the catastrophic drop in bookings during the Gulf War in 1991), the islands have done a remarkably good job, and tourism sits squarely as the cornerstone of the islands' economy.

Holidaymakers, mainly from Britain, France, Italy and Germany, bring in some Rs600 million annually (by far the largest single contribution to the nation's GDP), and 1993 was a record year for the industry on Seychelles. There are some 20 large hotels and another 70 smaller establishments and guest houses, mostly on Mahé, Praslin and La Digue. Although up to 100,000 visitors arrive each year, there can never be more than 4500 tourists at one time. The government is unlikely to allow this to rise much, as the islands have successfully concentrated on the higher paying tourist and established an image of exclusivity. The result of this is that apart from the occasional glimpse of a hotel pool through the trees, the proliferation of superb restaurants, and mini mokes touring the mountain roads, visitors are not in fact very noticeable. There seems to be a secluded corner of paradise for everyone.

FAMOUS VISITORS

Noel Coward. Had to spend a couple of nights in hospital. Complained about that and the fungus on his hotel wall.

Ian Fleming. May well have found inspiration for the underwater scenes in *Thunderball*, which he was writing at the time.

Ronald Reagan. Hollywood actor. Stayed on Praslin.

Archbishop Makarios of Cyprus. Less an exile than a relaxing holiday. Used to climb the mountains of Mahé in his flowing black robes.

Pope John Paul II. The islands are 97% Catholic, so his mass at Stade Populaire was well attended.

Queen Elizabeth II. Came to open the airport in 1971.

Fishing

Surrounded by so much ocean and coral reef, fishing has always been Seychelles' primary harvest, and although high-powered boats have taken over from wooden pirogues poled over the reef, fishing is still very much part of the life and culture. Some 6000 tonnes of fish are landed annually, and in addition 3000 tonnes of tuna are now processed each year at the new tuna cannery built on reclaimed land just outside Victoria. Shark, ray, octopus, and crab are all caught in large quantities, and both crayfish and prawns are farmed. Seychelles also sells fishing rights to the likes of Korea, Japan, and Russia.

Agriculture

To all those who dropped anchor in Seychelles' blue waters down the centuries, the islands were always regarded as a bountiful paradise. However, the natural resources suffered at the hands of those who came, as tortoises were a popular source of fresh meat and the tall trees highly valued as ship-building timber.

In general, the alkaline granite soil is not generous, and with labour scarce after the abolition of slavery, trying to grow anything on Seychelles for profit was at best a risky enterprise. Yet, as every successive and ultimately frustrated British administrator wrote back to the colonial office, more could always have been made of the potential. Plantations of **copra**, **cinnamon**, **patchouli** and **vanilla** all enjoyed short-lived booms at one time or another, but today these are all but derelict.

There have, however, been moves recently to establish a stronger agricultural base, and the government has shown

Below: *The ocean waters around Seychelles are rich fishing territory. Game fishing charters are a big draw for visitors.*

support. There are some substantial farms on Praslin, La Digue and Silhouette; Seychelles is self-sufficient in **tea** and **coffee**, and it produces all its own **chicken** and 40% of its **beef** requirements.

Above: *Cinnamon bark being put out to dry. Once a major part of Seychelles' economy, the spice industry has declined significantly.*

Brisk business

Given a solid base by the more settled latter years of Albert René's benign one-party rule, construction, manufacturing and business in Seychelles have flourished in the new light of democracy and international support.

Many businesses, such as restaurants and craft shops, benefit from the considerable spin-offs from tourism, but there are also architects, lawyers, boat-builders, dress makers, and excellent furniture makers doing well. There is a daily paper and at least three weeklies, and a broadcasting company, Radio Television Seychelles. Being an island, Mahé Shipping is a prosperous concern, while the presence of Cable and Wireless has ensured an excellent phone system, and quite a number of Seychellois own faxes. Seychelles appears in the Guinness Book of World Records as being the smallest nation to run its own international airline, Air Seychelles.

Being so far from export markets, and limited in resources, Seychelles does not manufacture a great deal. Tea, tuna, beer (Seybrew and Eku are the two local brands), soft drinks, and mineral water (from the Val Riche area of Mahé) are produced locally, although

PERFUMES

As if Seychelles didn't have enough connections with romance and exoticism, there have been attempts recently to establish a perfume industry on Mahé. *Kreolfleurage*, manufactured by German microbiologist Pit Hugelmann, has a range of three Seychelles fragrances using as much as 20% local content from plants picked on Morne Seychellois and at Police Bay. He makes use of the beautiful and varied frangipani before it falls, and hibiscus, the quintessential flower of the tropics, before it opens. Over 40 different essences go into *Bwanwar* (Blackwood) perfume including cinnamon bark, vetiver, vanilla, patchouli and passionfruit flower.

GETTING AHEAD

Seychelles is almost totally literate, with doctors, computer buffs, engineers, aircraft pilots, businessmen and teachers. Nearly one-third of the population is under 18 and there are 10,000 pupils in primary school and 7000 in secondary. There is a school for gifted children, a polytechnic offering business studies, engineering, art and design, and a hotel training school. The Seychellois nearly all speak English and French, and many speak Italian and German as well.

Above: *A strip of land reclaimed from the sea, towards the foreground, which has been created just to the south of Victoria.*
Below: *A general store on Mahé's backroads.*

SHADES OF SEYCHELLES

Colour hardly matters now in post-tourism boom Seychelles, although it used to. Someone of Indian descent was a *Malbar*, a very dark person a *Mazambik*, a European who had gone to seed a *blanc rouille coko* (white rusting among the coconuts). There are no more *grand blancs* (quasi-aristocratic French plantation owners); they have quietly exchanged a drop in status for the lucrative egalitarianism of tourism.

cigarettes, milk and fruit juices are reprocessed from imported stocks, which also provides employment. The fact that most importing is still done by the centralized Seychelles Marketing Board (SMB), with the resulting price controls and restrictions, still hampers enterprise and is reflected on the supermarket shelves. The government is still a large employer, and while there is no income tax, there are quite large business, trade and excise taxes. For the moment, however, the key remains whether tourism can be maintained to match the good life the Seychellois have come to accept as normal.

THE PEOPLE

Western writers have always described the Seychellois as smiling, happy-go-lucky folk straight out of a Gauguin painting. The Seychellois certainly know and take advantage of the paradise in which they live, and the climate and beauty make them fairly laid-back, but they are not beaming, brown-skinned natives in sarongs singing love songs as the long boats ride in on the surf. They are canny, wily island folk drawn from a mix of African, Malagasy, Indian, Chinese, and European roots who have developed a unique and adaptable culture. They have a great sense of fun and an irrepressible knack for gossiping; at every bus-stop, street corner, hotel and shop they will pass witty, but friendly, comments about you, your dress (or lack of it), and your spouse.

Above: *A line of smiling Seychellois siblings.*

The Seychellois can be welcoming, quick to offer help or to invite you home for a meal, and happy to share their knowledge of the islands. Tourism has changed their lives, but it has not trampled their spirit: at the least hint of arrogance or condescension they will freeze you out, and no-one can be more deaf than a hotel waitress whose pride has been affronted.

Family Life

Coming out of the times when slaves were not allowed to marry and any children automatically

---

USEFUL KREOL EXPRESSIONS

English is spoken by everyone in Victoria, and by all taxi drivers, hoteliers, restaurateurs and shop keepers. However, knowing a few words of Kreol will always win you a few friends:

Good morning, sir: *bonzour msye*
Where is the road, brother?: *Oli semen, mon frer?*
(From old French: Ou est le chemin, mon frère?)
Please tell me, madam, what time does the bus get here?: *Pardon, madam, ou capab di mwa, keler bis yarive?*
(Roughly from old French: Pardon, madame, vous êtes capable de dire moi, quelle heure l'autobus y arrive?)
May I use your toilet, please?: *Moi capab servi ou kabine si'ouple?*
Is there a shop over there?: *Yen enn boutik laba?*
I am going to... : *Mon pe al...*

Excuse me: *Ekskize*
Yes: *wi*
No: *non*
Do you speak English, madam?: *Ou koz Angle, madam?*
Hotel: *lotel*
I don't know: *mon pa konnen*
How much?: *konbyen sa?*
One: *enn*
Two: *de*
Three: *twa*
And, everyone's favourite words in Kreol:
kouyon: favourite expletive – used liberally to cover every situation, self-recrimination and motoring confrontation.
Bouldou or *kwavev*: the common term for sweetheart.

Above: *The tropical colours of the islands, inside a Mahé boutique.*

belonged to the master, a tradition of living *en ménage* (together) without marrying took root; as a result families tend to be rather loose, though by no means weak, arrangements. Children are commonly looked after by their mother alone. **Seychellois women** are confident, shrewd, and tend to be the fulcrum of society. There are more women in the Seychelles parliament than in any other country in the world, and they are the power behind many successful businesses.

Language

There is really no such thing as a Kreol (or Creole – as it is spelt in other parts of the world) person in Seychelles – rather everyone is Seychellois, and their national language is **Kreol**. The language is based on the French of slavery days, but it has strong African intonations and has, over the years, incorporated Malagasy, Indian, Arabic, and in recent years a good many English words. A French speaker will understand it, although to read it in its phonetic written form is difficult (and frequently amusing) at first.

Kreol is also spoken in Mauritius and in parts of the Caribbean, but Seychelles was the first country to develop it as a written medium and give it equal status as an official language. It is a living, changing language, and a Kreol Institute has been set up in Mahé to promote it. Primary schoolchildren used to be taught in Kreol although recently this has been changed to English. Business and law use English, those of French descent speak that language at home, and the news is read on television in all three.

Religion

The **Catholic** faith, to which 97% of the population are adherents, remains at the core of Seychellois culture. The menfolk, except at funerals, affect to treat that bond lightly, but there is no doubting the strength of it, and one of the images of the islands is the colourfully dressed worshippers on their way to their parish church on Sundays – men in starched white shirts, the older ladies with hats, and the young girls in their lovingly-sewn first communion dresses.

Above: *The colour and artistry of the Hindu temple in Victoria.*

Inside church, with the scent of eau de cologne and coconut cream wafting under the fans, the atmosphere is heady. The singing is excellent, especially at the three churches on Mahé served by 'the singing priest', Père Gustave Lafortune, while features such as the marquetry interior of Our Lady of Seven Sorrows at Anse Boileau, and the impressive altar windows of St Paul's in Victoria, are examples of art that can lift the spirit.

Below: *A prominent statue of the Virgin Mary, displaying the importance of the islands' Catholic heritage.*

There are beautiful grottoes along every remote road and tiny cove in Seychelles, and the bell tower of the church is the focal point of each tiny village. Many islanders still cross themselves passing a church, even if they're in a bus. Saints' feast days are grand events, with bunting, sports competitions, music and processions.

MUSIC MAN

Patrick Victor is a big dark man with a rose in his hat and sorrow in his eyes. Almost single-handedly he has rescued the folk music of Seychelles from extinction, especially the *moutia* music of the mountains and the poor. He grew up the eldest of nine children near the Nageant plantation in the country village of Pointe La Rue, which is now buried under the airport. His mission is 'to put the soul of the past into the present', and in doing so he has played all over Europe and Africa.

Very much in the minority, the other religions and denominations do have a presence. There are four Anglican churches in Seychelles; in Victoria there is a Hindu temple and a mosque; and there are also smart new Jehovah's Witness, Seventh Day Adventist and Apostolic churches. In the days before electricity there was substantial belief in *gris gris* (black magic), but with a young modern population it mainly exists today as folk memory and party banter.

Music and Dance

Apart from the mischievous Soungoula stories, there is very little Seychelles literature, though this may change with higher levels of literacy. The lush tropical atmosphere of Seychelles has always been an inspiration for artists, but it is music that truly captures the spirit of the islands, and no more so than the defiant, evocative *moutia*. High in the mountains or on a remote beach a slow chanting and sensuous shuffle dance would begin around a fire made from old coconut fronds, a line of men facing another of women, everyone else watching. Born in slave days, the *moutia* is pure Africa, the rumbling drum evoking anguished memories of another time. It was frowned upon by the establishment, who were seldom invited to the all-night rave-ups, and naughty children would get a hiding from parents for sneaking a peak. These days a visitor will only see the dance at a folk festival, or where friends play for each other's enjoyment.

Below: *Sega dancing – sensual, striking, and straight from the deeply-rooted Kreol tradition.*

The sega, on the other hand, is in every hotel for every visitor, and nowadays is often exuberantly danced with colourful

Mauritian costumes. The islanders' (and some would say more wicked) version is danced with small, rhythmic steps and a much subtler sway in the hips, neither partner ever touching.

Family dances and weddings are jolly affairs, with violins, banjo, accordian, triangle, and drums providing the music for *kamtole* – Seychelles waltzes, polkas, masok and contredanse, performed with shouted instructions from a *komander*, rather like country and western.

The two leading musicians in Seychelles are Patrick Victor, a *moutia* poet and folksinger, and the classically trained David Andre. You will hear Andre's *nostalgie* music as you board Air Seychelles; the exquisite violin is by Xu Lu, a Seychellois of Chinese descent. Others include the 10-strong Sokwe group, with much colourful chorus dancing, the 'Vendredi Saint' *moutia* of Jean Marc Volcy, and Jenny Letourdi.

No-one, however, has reached the standing of old folk hero Tonpa, legendary master of the Seychelles *bonm* (bow and gourd). Above the fountain at the La Bastille National Archives in Victoria there is a bust of Tonpa and two friends on the *zez, bonm* and *tambour* (drum), playing, as the old *moutia* song goes, ' ... until dawn breaks, and its time to milk the goats'.

> ### NATURAL RHYTHMS
>
> The traditional musical instruments of Seychelles are made from various local materials. These include:
> - a hollowed out calabash as a sounding box in both the *zez* and *bonm*.
> - a bamboo cone, and strings from bamboo bark used to make a *mouloumba*, a cross between a megaphone and a violin.
> - the *tamtam* is a hollowed-out tree trunk. The *tambour* is made from a roundel of *Karambol* wood. A manta ray or goat skin is then stretched over this and heated to maximise resonance.

Below: *The wonderful cuisine of Seychelles is an essential guide to understanding, and appreciating, the true tropical appeal of the islands.*

Island Cuisine

With a heritage drawing from French, Indian, Chinese, and Kreol roots, the quality of the cuisine in Seychelles could only be wonderful. Few menus fail to be mouthwatering. The staples of the Seychellois diet are *kordonnyen* fish, rice, coconut, breadfruit, chillies, spices and mangoes, each of them cooked in a hundred different and delicious ways.

Right: *Breadfruit and plantain side by side.*
Opposite top: *A paraglider standing by for take-off over Beau Vallon Bay.*
Opposite bottom: *A golfer on the palm-lined, manicured fairways of the course at Anse aux Pins.*

THE BREADFRUIT TREE

The story has it that if you eat breadfruit in Seychelles you'll always come back. These dark green trees grow all over Seychelles. Its leaves are rather like giant oak leaves, and the green cannon-ball fruits make great eating. When ripe they weigh in at 3kg (7lb) and fall in a yellow mush to the ground; cut them down with a long stick and catch them (if you're clever) before they fall and serve fried, mashed, or made into a pudding with coconut milk. Best of all, eat it baked whole over an open wood fire. It is supposed to be the Tree of Life and everyone has a tree in their garden. The texture is breadlike, though it is not made into bread. 'A poor substitute for potatoes', one writer in 1940 sniffed. The wood from the tree makes good floor planking.

Indian dhal or yellow lentils are commonly made into a thick soup, while saffron rice is served with an onion, orange and spices salad as a picnic pilau with grilled suckling pig. Various types of seafood are always popular, among them grilled *bouzwa* snapper fish, cold *zob* fish, and fresh *tectec* clams dug up from the beach, and made into a soup. Other delicacies are *satini rekin* (dried shark chutney), smoked sailfish and fruit bat, but perhaps nothing beats the simplest rice and salted fish in a banana frond pouch, fisherman style.

For dessert, go for bananas fried in brown sugar or pineapple in red wine. A few of the other delights are manioc (cassava) as a pudding cooked in freshly grated coconut, sweet potatoes in honey, or wild *framboises* from the mountains of La Misère. Sweets are made of pamplemousse peel, jams from zamalak fruit, and popular snacks are *gato pimen* chillibites and *nouga koko*.

Wines are expensive and the French selection isn't always great. Try *kalou* (coconut tree toddy), or, for a real blast, *bacca* rum. Lemon grass or citronelle tea helps the digestion. There are a number of excellent restaurants around the islands, but, if the opportunity arises, never turn up the chance of home cooking.

Sport and Recreation

People tend to wake up with the six o'clock sun, so wild all-hours revelling is not common, though the hotels with their discos, casinos, coffee shops and barbecues have replaced much of the home entertainment, which is usually folksy accordion singsongs and dancing. After church on Sunday, the done thing is a boat trip and picnic out on one of the smaller islands near Mahé.

Sitting on an upturned bucket on the beach to the ferocious slapping of dominoes is a regular rite all through the islands. It is universally addictive among men, along with football and athletics, the two main sports in which Seychelles competes internationally. More recently, swimming, diving, sailing and windsurfing have become popular among the islanders, and there is now a sail training school in Victoria. Seychellois are also keen on boxing, basketball and volleyball.

In Seychelles everyone is a fisherman, and making friends with the

pêcheur nearest your beach could avoid the cost of big sea charters. Golf is played, mainly by visitors at the nine hole Reef golf course, where the hazards include falling coconuts and crabs with a reputation for stealing balls. You can ride horses on La Digue, paraglide at Beau Vallon, play tennis, and find all the regular water sports at most big hotels.

OCTOPUS CURRY

Octopus curry is the national dish of Seychelles. Wash the octopus and beat the poor old fellow with a rolling pin for 15 minutes, then boil for an hour in water. Slice the flesh very fine. Season with two teaspoons of curry powder, pepper, salt, two onions, a touch of chilli and two cinnamon leaves. Add three cups of coconut cream and cook for 30 minutes. Serve with rice and heart of palm salad (also called 'millionaire's salad', as it takes the centre of one palmiste palm to make each salad).

2
North Mahé

Mahé is the largest and most important of the widely spread islands of Seychelles, only 27km (17 miles) long but given an impressive, brooding presence by a backbone of high forested mountains. These granitic peaks are the highest in the archipelago, and a distinguishing feature since they were first sighted by Arab seamen. Mahé was the site of the first French landings in 1742, and the first settlement in 1770. Today 90% of the population of Seychelles lives on the island, with a large proportion of that figure in the nation's capital, **Victoria**.

Around Mahé's coastline there are 75 beaches and coves (known as 'anse' in Seychelles), ranging from long, sweeping stretches of sand, to isolated little bays tucked among granite cliffs and thick green trees. Except for the western corner, a narrow and twisting tarred road rings the island; it fringes sea, reef and an overgrown coconut jungle dotted with hidden and often precariously perched Kreol houses.

The side of Mahé to the northeast of the central range of mountains encompasses the three most important single locations on the island: the **airport** at Point La Rue, the capital, Victoria, and **Beau Vallon Bay**, the principal tourist area. Victoria is the main harbour in Seychelles, and the heart of business and commerce. It rises quickly into the mountains, through leafy suburbs such as Bel Air and Bel Eau; driving north, the land soon becomes rural, although it is not until the crushed coral beach of North East Point that you reach the first whispering palms and

CLIMATE

The sea and winds keep Mahé refreshed. **Humidity** is around 80% all year, but can reach 85%. To some extent the buildings and paved roads of Victoria hold in the heat, and make it hotter than the rural and mountain areas. **Temperature** is 80°F (27°C) year round, with only a slight drop at night. **Rain** falls heavily from November to March but drops to as low as 70mm (3in) in June.

Opposite: *The centre of attraction. Beau Vallon beach, with Silhouette dominating the horizon.*

Above: *Victoria harbour in the foreground, with the town among the thick foliage behind.*

rumbling reef. Mahé's top beach, Beau Vallon, is only a 15 minute drive over the mountain saddle from Victoria, while huddled in the wide bay of the eastern coastline are a group of small islands that are incorporated in **St Anne's Marine National Park**, a kaleidoscopic garden of underwater life.

VICTORIA

From the air or the sea Victoria seems to be lost in a green jungle beneath the towering black cliffs of Trois Frères. The first French inhabitants were attracted to the sheltered anchorage, but the land must have seemed an impenetrable swathe of mangrove swamp. The settlement was initially called L'Etablissement, before becoming Victoria in 1841 in honour of the Queen. It is the seat of government, the location of most of the main institutions and businesses, and the only centre in the 115 islands that can really be described as a town.

Victoria's size has been substantially increased in recent years by land reclamation, which has allowed the development of the New Port, the airport, a large tuna cannery, a sports complex, new factories, and clusters of housing, as well as the only stretch of road in Seychelles where cars can reach 80kph (50mph). Still, it is one of the smallest capitals in the world – you can stroll from one end of town to the other in ten minutes. *Tata* buses and pedestrians dodge and weave through the streets, colourful, corrugated tin chateaux with drooping balconies stand defiantly beside chunky modern buildings, while along the tree-lined pavements life is always bustling with noisy street stalls and closely-packed shops.

DON'T MISS

*** Beau Vallon Beach: the definitive Seychelles beach, only 15 minutes over the mountain road from Victoria.
*** Victoria Walkabout: start at the Clock Tower, and take in all the sights, sounds, and smells of the islands' charming capital.
*** St Anne Marine National Park: just off Victoria, a feast of coral and fish. See it from the comfort of a glass semisubmersible.
** Botanical Gardens: a downtown taste of the spectacular Seychelles flora. Coco de mer, tortoises and lunch.
** The Market: everything exotic for sale and some great personalities.
** Game Fishing: boats from Marine Charter next to the yacht club. You don't have to go too far to find the ocean.
* National Museum: fascinating historic Seychelles.
*Art Gallery: inside the National Library. All the best of Seychelles' talented artists.

A Walk around the Clock ★★★

Victoria is small enough that it doesn't take long to see everything on foot. You quickly pick up the chirpiness of the Seychellois and the relaxed tropical feel of the place. The focal point of town is the **Clock Tower**, erected in 1903 to mark Seychelles' coming of age as a separate colony. Before land reclamation it stood on the harbour front: Independence Avenue, leading out to the harbour, was Long Pier, while Francis Rachel Street going off to the south was the promenade along the harbour wall.

Starting at the Clock Tower, set off along Francis Rachel – it was named after one of the two people killed during the coup d'état – towards the roundabout at **Le Chantier** to the southeast. An avenue of shady trees and flowers, the avenue runs past the court house, the **Stade Populaire** (People's Stadium), and the old tin-roofed shops of Temooljees, Adam Moosa, and Chaka Brothers. These are food, cloth and hardware merchants which date back to colonial days when they were the islands' bankers, offering 'indefinite credit and unfailing courtesy'. Their sons and grandsons still greet you with old world politesse as you enter, even if you can no longer buy a bottle of home-made lemonade with a marble stopper. A nearby disco marks the multi-coloured, two-storey **museum** of the ruling SPPF (Seychelles People's Progressive Front) party. Across the street, just past the law courts with the attractive bust of spices pioneer Pierre Poivre (Peter Pepper) outside, is the town's only petrol station, and the scene of traffic jams at four o'clock every afternoon.

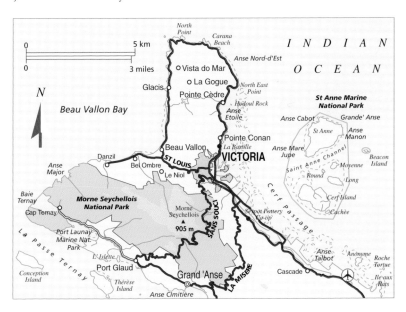

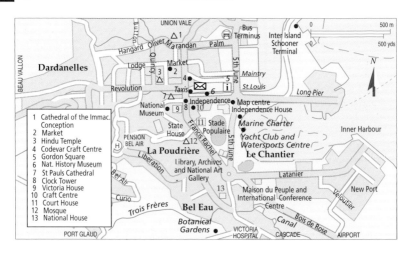

Map legend:
1 Cathedral of the Immac. Conception
2 Market
3 Hindu Temple
4 Codevar Craft Centre
5 Gordon Square
6 Nat. History Museum
7 St Pauls Cathedral
8 Clock Tower
9 Victoria House
10 Craft Centre
11 Court House
12 Mosque
13 National House

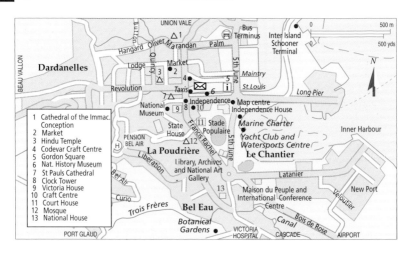

WHERE THE CLOCK CHIMES TWICE

There is a clock that chimes in Victoria, but it isn't the Clock Tower in the middle of town. A crucial part was lost over the side of the ship as the commemorative clock was unloaded in 1903, and no-one could make the bell work after that. What you will hear chiming is the clock in the Roman Catholic Cathedral, beyond the market. When the travel writer Alec Waugh (brother of the novelist Evelyn) came to Seychelles, he wrote a book called 'Where the Clock Chimes Twice'. And why does it chime twice? One version is that the first is to wake everyone up, and the second to tell them the time.

The ultramodern facilities of Cable and Wireless are alongside the old grey and white colonial facade of **Kenwyn House**, a national monument. Nearby is the **Mosque** of Sheikh Mohamed bin Khalifa. Carry on past the **New Library** with its Grecian columns and you come to the huge dark trees marking Le Chantier fountain and roundabout, the site of the old boatbuilding yard and gateway to **New Port**.

Opposite along Latanier Road is the **National Assembly**, or *Maison du Peuple*, partly hidden by trees, and beyond it the power station and port office. Continue the walk by doubling back along 5th June Avenue (the day of the coup in 1977 – known as Liberation Day) towards the town centre, passing **La Vev music recording studio**, then the **yacht club**, with halyards clattering in the breeze, and the **Marine Charter quay**. The conspicuous **Zom Libre statue**, commemorating the events of 1977, is on the other side of the road.

There is another statue in the middle of the roundabout on Independence Avenue, a threesome of soaring fairy terns. A left turn here will take you past the helpful **Tourist Office** in Independence House, and then back to the Clock Tower, while to the right is the wide new road leading to the fishing port. The inter-island schooner terminal and its port-side restaurant are at the northern end of this forked road. The view here is impressive as you look out across the Cerf Passage, often with large tuna fishing boats anchored in it, to the string of islands in St Anne Marine National Park. Some of the larger cruise ships will still moor out in the roads, where in earlier days young men would dive 18m (60ft) to the seabed to be rewarded with coins.

National Museum *

A pair of cannon, green with age, flank the entrance to the National Museum, situated opposite the street craft stalls on Independence Avenue in the centre of town. Inside, glass cabinets and displays hoard all manner of strange objects, including pirates' pistols, old Seychelles musical instruments, giant clams used for holy water outside churches, crocodile skulls, and stuffed tortoises. Two massive chunks of granite stand in the entrance hall. One is the Possession Stone, the symbol of French claim to the islands, and the other an old pirate's tombstone inscribed with skull and crossbones, which reads: 'Jean-Pierre Le Chartier, killed on March 4, 1805 by his friend Evellon. Passersby pray for me'. Whether for pirate or his murderer is left unsaid. The Museum will be moving soon to the Old Library on State House Avenue.

> **STONE OF POSSESSION**
>
> Seychelles' oldest monument, the Stone of Possession, has had an eventful life. Erected by Irish-French Captain Corneille Nicholas Morphey on the shores of Victoria in 1756 to signify the French claim to the islands, it was supposed to have lain neglected in the garden of the brothel in La Poudière Lane for many years. Someone had an idea that it should go to a museum in Paris, and it wasn't until it reached Aden on the Red Sea that it was intercepted and returned. It then stood in the grounds of State House for a while, before being moved to take pride of place in the National Museum.

Below: *The daring new National Library and Art Gallery in Victoria.*

National Library and Art Gallery *

Built by public subscription and opened in 1994 the three-storey National Library belongs to a school of architecture which can only be described as gothic tropic. It is a truly wonderful *folie de grandeur*, all lego tiles, Grecian columns and soaring space. Future generations will no doubt applaud its construction

SEYCHELLES ARTISTS

The islands can boast a range of excellent artists. See them in the National Art Gallery, or pay a visit to their studio.
- **Michael Adams**. Perhaps the most famous Seychelles painter. Colour, people and activity, and much imitated.
- **Christine Harter**. From Praslin. She painted the huge mural in the foyer of the Beau Vallon Bay Hotel.
- **Serge Rouillon**. Attractive portraits, little houses tucked away in the greenery.
- **Verney Cresswell**. Beach scenes in watercolour.
- **Leon Bacco**. Excellent wood carvings.

but query its strange architecture, a subject which quickly raises heated debate in Seychelles.

Inside, however, it is lovely. There are not a great many books, but it has an unhurried reference department, and it is a wonderful home for Seychelles art. The Seychellois are not great novelists or poets, but they are fine artists. If the 1994 grand opening exhibition is anything to go by, Seychelles can look very optimistically towards its creative future. The rooms are awash with guache, acrylics, oils, and watercolours. Woodsculptures by Tom Bowyers and Liz Rouillon's plant studies are worth seeking out, as are Michael Adam's colourful paintings and those by Vladimir Tarakanoff and Christine Harter.

Shopping

Start at **La Kaz craft shop** and the **street stalls** near the Clock Tower for a wide variety of simple, locally-made items such as delicately hand-painted wooden keyrings of coral fish, conical Seychellois fisherman's hats, and shopping bags woven from coco de mer, raffia and sisal palm fronds. Be wary, however, of the seashells and mother of pearl offered for sale, as they've been taken from the sea to be sold there, as well as the 'tortoiseshell' ornaments made from the endangered hawksbill turtles.

Market Street is the real hub for shopping in Victoria. You can buy packets of tea, spices, coconut cream, crochet work and even the local liqueur, *Coco d'Amour*. **Jivan's** on the corner of Albert and Market has a good selection of cloth, and Kanti, the owner, is worth chatting to. He is a fellow of the Royal Geographical Society and an expert on Seychelles, as is his son. Nearby you can find Seychelles palm frond baskets, **Ray's**

Music Room with a good selection of Patrick Victor's folk music, and some crazily coloured T-shirts in **Sunstroke**. Pop into the little **general merchants** with names like Sham Peng Tong, Chetty, Pillay, or Kim Koon, and buy anything from a box of matches to a video camera.

Maps of the different islands can be obtained from the **Survey Office** 50m (55yd) from the *Twa Zwazo* (three birds) fountain and there is a good **bookshop**, Antigone, in the arcade up from Air Seychelles. There is a philatelic counter at the **post office**, and 200m (220yd) beyond it along Albert Street is **Codevar,** the main crafts co-op.

Victoria Market ★★

The Market is hard to miss under a panoply of mango and flame trees as you walk up Market Street. Started in 1839, it is sometimes to referred to as Sir Selwyn Clarke Market, after the post-World War II governor. It is open every day except Sunday, with Saturday being particularly hectic. The best time to be there is when the fish are heaved in, and though crowded and noisy, it is safe. Ask, however, if you want to take a picture of someone.

The market is a hive of all things strange and exotic. You can buy such things as *bouzwa* red snapper heads for soups, pale green chilli-like *sousout*, or *patole* (a sort of hollow cucumber), *zamalak* fruits, mangoes (ripe or unripe), *fatak* reed brooms, coconut graters, and chillies, the smaller the hotter.

Opposite: *The Clock Tower, looking south.*
Above: *Streetside stalls near the Clock Tower.*

BEST BUYS
● Colourfully painted wooden fish **keyrings**. ● Seychelles palm weave **baskets and bags**. ● **Hats** – which come in all shapes and colours. ● **Postcards**. Superb photography and printing. ● David Andre or Patrick Victor **CDs** (*nostalgie* and *tambour moutia* respectively). ● **Spices** – before they get to a glass jar. ● **Teas** – especially citronelle or vanilla. ● **Jewellry** by Lorna Delorie. ● A whisky miniature of **chillies** from Mr Lolo Adrienne in the market.

Above: *Market Street.*

The best part of the market, however, is near the back where some wonderful characters keep their stalls. Look out for the diminutive Joseph Lolo Adrienne's bottled jams and chutneys, where he explains with all the tricks and treats of a medicine man how to cook with his special curry powders and hellfire sauces. Or try speaking a few words of Kreol to Yvonne Sidoney at her fruit, vegetable and *gallette mayok* (a crusty biscuit made of manioc) stall, and you'll make a lifelong friend. Shoo away the white egrets, which are called *Madam Paton* by the locals (after a white haired lady who bore a resemblance), as you taste some of the wonderful delicacies.

The Botanical Gardens **

Industrial wealth, a far-flung empire and botanist Charles Darwin's studies on the evolution of living things caused an explosion of interest in birds and bees in Victorian Britain. One outcome was Kew Gardens in London; another – if not quite so grand – was the Botanical Gardens in Seychelles.

The entrance to the Botanical Gardens is less than a mile south of town, opposite the Democratic Party Headquarters and adjacent to the hospital. Coco de mer palms dominate the path up into the Gardens. Other

endemic palms by the path include *latanier*, which is used for thatching, and *palmiste*, the favourite ingredient for millionaire's salad.

Above: *The colonial elegance of State House and its gardens.*

The Gardens lie in a granite-humped, grassy strip between two small streams trickling down from the massif that soars above the trees. Water lilies, papyrus, and even some tiny fish and transparent shrimps can be spotted here. The 6ha (15 acres) Gardens were established nearly 100 years ago and owe a lot to its original Director, Rivaltz Dupont, who travelled the world gathering exotic trees and plants. Many of the unusual trees are labelled, there is a nursery for young plants, an orchid garden, a large tortoise pen formed by natural black boulders, a small aviary, and a restaurant set beneath Norfolk Pines. The hospital next door has a lovely enclosed quadrangle, and up at the top of the hill you might find some fruit bats hanging upside down from the trees.

The Headquarters of Seychelles National Parks are situated in the Gardens, where the scientists are informed, dedicated, and helpful. Theirs is the task of conserving Seychelles' unparalleled natural heritage. At the entrance to the Gardens there is a car park and a latticed rondavel with information leaflets.

STATE HOUSE

Completed in 1913, this gracious residence of colonial governors and presidents is sited on a small rise just above town on the way up to Bel Air. An avenue of towering sandragon trees leads up to its manicured lawns and open expanses of flowering trees. It was designed by Lady William Davidson, the wife of one of the governors, though she neglected to include in her design a staircase for the two-storeyed house, a fact that was only discovered mid-construction. It has lofty white columns and long verandahs with roll down split bamboo blinds for the rain, and an elegant interior. Access is by permission only. Queau de Quincy's tomb is in the grounds.

Above: *The dramatic bleeding heart flower.*

Cemetery

3km (2 miles) from town along the road to the south is Seychelles' main cemetery. Cemeteries may not be a common choice for a stroll, but this one has such an attractive swathe of bumpy grass, black granite and open mountain scenery that it deserves being the exception. Turn right 100m past Photo Eden in Mont Fleuri opposite the little shops that hang over the side of the road.

There is nothing organised about the layout: the ground, a gently rising hill, is too uneven for that. White crosses mix with coral walls and the occasional imposing, lopsided mausoleum. The inscriptions are often in French – the language always reserved for formal occasions – but Kreol is found too on the home-made crosses.

From the road at the top of the cemetery, there is a scenic walk back to town. It runs past Rochon, where women wash clothes in the river, slapping them against boulders and holding raucous conversations across from one level to the next. Under a tangled spaghetti of electricity and telephone wires, festooned with the webs of giant black and brown palm spiders, mynah birds yabber away as noisily as the washerwomen. A narrow footbridge beneath a dark canopy of trees crosses into the aptly named Forêt Noire (Black Forest). Not long after the forest there are views of the emerald waters of the harbour, with boats milling around the dock, and St Anne's Island beyond. To complete the walk cut left up Liberation Road just before National House to Bel Eau, which seems steep until you come to another grand vista of the town. From here it is no more than 15 minutes walk back into town.

AROUND VICTORIA
Coastal Road South

The old main road south from Victoria is a charming, twisting route through a green jungle with old houses dotted on one side of the road, and the sea on the other. There are plenty of cars and buses going along it, although a pleasant option is to walk it.

After the cemetery at **Mont Fleuri** you'll come to the **La Misère** mountain pass roundabout. Staying on the coast road you pass the church of **St Thérèse**, **Gerard Devoud's art gallery**, the **Seypot Pottery co-op**, the derelict island schooner (and former restaurant) *Isle of Farquhar*, and then the bridge across the small **Mamelles River**. This used to mark the beginning of town in the old days, the start of dim street lights where you put on your shoes for the big city. It is also the site of the oldest and possibly the most elegant plantation house in the islands, **Chateau des Mamelles**. Built in 1804, and formerly the residence of 'Le Corsair' Jean François Hodoul, it is now a national monument.

> **AVALANCHE**
>
> On the night of 12 October 1862 a huge avalanche descended on Victoria, with 100 tonne granite blocks rolling down the mountains, followed by a sea of mud which killed 75 people. For many years after the Seychellois measured time 'before or after the avalanche'. It created a flat area of ground which was used as the town's football field. Later it became Gordon Square (after General 'Chinese' Gordon), now called Freedom Square.

Below: *A view from Plaisance up to Mahé's high central backbone of mountains.*

Below: *Cascade's dominant old church steeple.*
Opposite: *Massed granite stolidity on the shore of the northern peninsula.*

Cascade

Past the busy Seychelles **brewery** is **Souverains des Mers**, where there is a permanent exhibition of 40 model ships, then Cascade, with its old water mill and pool. In the old days it was the choice mackerel fishing venue; today you can almost touch the jumbo jets coming in to land at the **airport** nearby.

The elegant church steeple, another national monument, dominates the village of Cascade. There's a track flanking the river into the hills which leads to pleasant waterfalls. Past the church the road runs along a narrow causeway before reaching the airport, built in 1971 on reclaimed land, which opened the way for the islands to develop tourism as its dominant industry.

The alternative route from Victoria is along the new **Bois de Rose Avenue**, built on reclaimed land. On the left is the seawall, with the afternoon wind whipping the tops off the waves, and on the right small skiffs in the serpentine lagoon that borders garden walls. Seychelles hardwoods have been planted along this new wide road to supercede the forest of casuarinas which were planted to help bond the coral dust which was used for land fill. There are some lovely views of mountain and mangrove shore, and keep an eye out for fiddler crabs at low tide.

Northern Peninsula

The road north from Victoria winds past **Radio Seychelles**, **La Bastille National Archives**, and the **Christian Far Eastern Broadcasting Association** (FEBA) with its red and white aerials marching out to sea, reaching **Anse Etoile**. During World War II British troops were quartered here, and although a bunker still juts defiantly out to sea, the Nazi submarines never came. Part of the bay was nicknamed 'smelly corner' after a U-shaped cove was filled in with refuse; it occasionally still lives up to its reputation.

MOUNTAINEERING CROCODILES

Early French settlers, lonely and frightened, would lie in their beds at night and, as the palms bent and clattered in the turbulent winds, thought they heard crocodiles doing battle with monster sharks in the storm-tossed bay. These same Nile crocodiles which lurked in the mangrove swamps were also reputed to climb the mountains of Mahé, hunting tortoises. The huge beasts were soon exterminated.

Following the road around this northerly peninsula of Mahé the whole central massif is visible, with views back to Victoria and its port, the 'golf balls' of the mountain tracking station at La Misère, and across the bay to the coral reefs around St Anne's Island.

The reef at **North East Point** is closer to the shore than at any other beach in Seychelles. If you want to take a closer look wear a pair of shoes and explore it at low tide. Otherwise take a stroll along the shell-strewn beach with its fringe of palms and casuarinas. The bay is not particularly good for swimming, and there is a wildness about the area, exposed as it is to the ocean and the northerly monsoon winds.

There is another walk here over the low hills from Anse Etoile, past Mahé's main reservoir, to the village of **Glacis**, which has a string of hotels and a historic church. There are two little Seychelles villages in the hills, **Maldive** and **La Gogue,** each with a cluster of breadfruit, mango and palm trees. The road is tarred as far as the reservoir, but only certain cars would be able to make it, so check carefully before you try. You can park at the Manresa guest house in Anse Etoile.

St Anne Marine National Park ★★★

The largest of Mahé's offlying islands are the group facing Victoria within the boundary of St Anne's Marine National Park. **St Anne's**, a mountain pyramid of an island right in front of Victoria harbour, was the site of the first French settlement 220 years ago. In those days the island was surrounded by mangroves, crocodiles roamed its forests, and dugongs swam off its quiet shores. A whaling station was set up there in 1832, while during World War II a giant petroleum storage tank was constructed to service seaplanes. Both the blubber boiler and the tank still stand forlorn and rusting away beneath the palms on the island. St Anne's is a restricted area as it is now the

headquarters for the Marine National Park.

Jumbos coming into land at the airport have one of the best views of the park. The water is a kaleidoscope of blue, turquoise, opal and aquamarine amongst the coral reefs, submarine islands of seaweed and the open flats of white sand which fringe these pretty islands.

The waters of the park are shallow, safe, and rich in coral and sealife. The best underwater areas for fish and coral are off Anse Cimitière and Cabot on St Anne, and in a stretch running between **Moyenne** and **Round Island**. The park and its islands are popular for day trips, with up to 35,000 people visiting it annually. One of the most interesting ways to see the spectacular underwater scenery is on a boat with a special glass keel, in which you can sit and marvel at the wonders of the reef on the other side of a window. There is a

DIVING

There are 10 dive centres in the islands, five of which are members of the Association of Professional Divers in Seychelles (APDS). Qualified PADI instructors will teach you, starting in the pool of a large hotel. The best times for diving and exploring the rich coral reefs around the islands are between April and May and again from October to November. Most dives are in the 10-20m (33-66ft) category from small boats near inshore reefs. For the big adventure the qualified diver can try the incredible coral walls in the Amirantes. Sharks have never been a problem in Seychelles. The islands host an annual Underwater Festival.

Above: *A glass-bottomed boat in the St Anne National Marine Park.*
Right: *The large stripy fish in the foreground is known as an oriental sweetlips.*

Conservation Information Centre on Round Island, and **restaurants** on Cerf, Round and Moyenne. With a pirate's grave hidden amongst the undergrowth, the latter is another prime site for trading treasure tales.

Above: *The spectacular, sweeping crescent of sand at Beau Vallon.*

BEAU VALLON ★★★

A beautiful valley couched between high mountains, Beau Vallon opens out onto a 6km (4 mile) bay stretching from Sunset Beach to the north all the way round to the granite cliffs of Bel Ombre, and incorporates an exquisite, mile-long, scimitar beach. Shaded by huge takamaka trees, whose fruit look like green pingpong balls, the white sandy beach is only 15 minutes over the mountains from Victoria, and has always been Seychelles' playground. There are half a dozen hotels around the bay, and it is the heart of action fun: paragliding, parachuting, water-skiing and diving are all on offer. For those less energetic all the poolside drinks have chilled sugar rimmed glasses, and the sunsets behind Silhouette Island are stunning.

The days when the Fairhaven Hotel would proudly advertise its running hot water and electricity have

> **GLIMPSES OF SEYCHELLES**
>
> These are a few of the best viewpoints in the north of the island.
> • **Sans Souci**: the road out of Victoria towards Morne Seychellois National Park. A number of excellent viewpoints over the harbour, islands and town.
> • **Le Niol**: if paragliding from the beach isn't your thing, this is the best view over Beau Vallon Bay.
> • **Pirate's Arms Hotel**: the best verandah in town for watching the laid-back life of Victoria go by.
> • **747**: it feels like you are about to land in the sea, but it makes for a great first glimpse of paradise.

TAMARIND AND ZAMALAKS

Year round there are fruits to be picked in Seychelles. You will see fallen fruit everywhere: on the roads, the mountains, and in everyone's backyard. They include:

• Tamarind. Tangy, tasty fruit, like a brown brittle pea-shell. Makes a lovely drink.

• Karambol. Tart star-shaped fruit. The wood makes the best roundel for tambourine-shaped *moutia* drums.

• Jackfruit. Grows on the trunk of trees. As big as a water melon. Very rich and strong smelling.

• Red-skinned bananas. Big and fat. *Banan mille* are tiny breakfast treats. Huge *banan zak* for cooking. There are 25 varieties in Seychelles.

• Mango. The Indian king of fruits. Unripe it is made into delicious salad with oil, vinegar, salt and pepper.

• Zamalak. White or red crispy fruits. Looks like a small apple. Good in jams and stewed.

passed, as these days paradise has to include swimming pools, tennis courts, boutiques, coffee shops, dancing, and watersports. Yet, for all that, even the largest hotels are hidden among the trees and you will never see more than 200 people on the beach.

One Man on a Dead Man's Chest

Near the saddle of the pass on the road from Victoria to Beau Vallon, a road twisting off to the left leads up through the granite massif and dark breadfruit forest to Le Niol, which has sweeping, lonely views of the whole of Beau Vallon Bay.

Down below, at the far western end of the crescent, is the beach and famous pirate treasure dig site at Bel Ombre. It seems terribly disappointing that a decent haul of treasure hasn't been found in Seychelles, as every palm laced cove and azure beach seems to hint of hidden plunder, and there were certainly plenty of pirates, privateers and corsairs knocking around the islands down the years. Many of their descendents still live in the islands.

Grenadier Guardsman **Reginald Cruise-Wilkins** came from England to settle at Beau Vallon in 1949 determined to find the treasure of cutthroat **Olivier le Vasseur**. *La Buse*, or the Buzzard, who ravaged the Indian Ocean in the 1770s, supposedly buried treasure

worth £100 million at Bel Ombre before he felt the gallows noose tighten around his neck. He is said to have tossed a scrap of paper to the crowd on the scaffold, calling, 'My treasure to he who will understand'. It was this cryptogram, based partially on the labours of Hercules, that Cruise-Wilkins believed he had mastered. Working with other documents supplied by locals, and encouraged by digs that had revealed strange rock markings and the corpses of two men with earrings, he spent decades and considerable amounts of money digging, constructing sea dykes and removing rock. But with the exception of a few tantalising clues: the trigger guard of a musket, a coin of Charles I's time, the stone statue of a woman, and a cavern with a trapdoor, he died disappointed. A pirate's flag used to fly over this corner of Bel Ombre by the side of the road where Cruise-Wilkins laboured for many years, and though the site is desolate, Cruise-Wilkins' son, John, has not yet abandoned hope.

Off the western end of Bel Ombre there is a walking path leading into Morne Seychellois National Park, which traverses the cliff tops to a pretty little cove called **Anse Major**, the wildest area of North Mahé.

DON'T EAT THE CRABS

Marianne North, the indomitable Victorian artist and botanist, whose superb paintings of flowers and plants hang in a special house in Kew Gardens, landed on North Mahé in 1883. She dropped her bag and screamed with wonder at the fiddler crabs 'to the amazement of my porters who said cooly they were not good to eat'.

Opposite: *Cerf Island, with Long Island and Moyenne behind, which form the southern part of St Anne National Marine Park.*
Below: *The church of St Roch, at Bel Ombre.*

North Mahé at a Glance

The cooler, drier months in Seychelles are during the southeast trades from **April to September.** At all times of year, however, it is tropically warm and humid. It can rain at any time, but expect torrential downpours lasting several days over the **Christmas** period.

Seychelles airport is 10km south of Victoria. It is served by **Air Seychelles** flights from Nairobi, London, Paris, Frankfurt, Rome, Madrid, Singapore, Johannesburg and other destinations en route. **Air France** links Seychelles to the Indian Ocean islands of Mauritius and Réunion, while **British Airways**, **Aeroflot** and **Kenya Airways** all have flights to Seychelles. **Transfers** from the airport are normally by tour operators, and sometimes hotels. There are also taxis (approx. Rs60 from the airport to Victoria).

Hire cars are by far the most popular way to explore the island. **Mini mokes** are perennial favourites, but remember that some of the mountain roads are steep. Try Hertz, tel: 322447, or any of a number of companies. **Motorbikes and bicycles** can also be hired. Try St Louis Motor Hire, tel: 266270. There is a regular and cheap **bus** service round the island, though it is a daylight service

only. The main bus station is near the harbour shore in Victoria, at the corner of Palm Street and June 5th Avenue. **Taxis** tend not to have meters, and are about 15 times the price of a bus. Check the fare first.

There are no large hotels in Victoria itself, as they all tend to be closer to the beaches.
Near Victoria:
MAIN HOTELS
Auberge Louis XVII. Up La Misère mountain, overlooking harbour. Cabanas, pool; tel: 344411, fax: 344428.
Pension Bel Air. Delightfully cool, grey and white colonial building overlooking Victoria. Family-run and very relaxed; tel: 224416, fax: 224923.
Sunrise. Guest house 100m south of Botanical Gardens; tel: 224560, fax: 225290.

BUDGET ACCOMMODATION
Beaufond Lane Guest House. Mont Fleuri, 1.5km south of town; tel: 224566.
La Louise. Not far from Auberge Louis XVII on La Misère; tel: 344349.
Hilltop. Just above Victoria; tel: 266555, fax: 266505.
Mountain Rise. On Sans Souci Rd. Antique colonial furniture, pool, panoramic views; tel: 225145, fax: 225503.

SELF CATERING
Michel Holiday Apartments. Just south of Victoria; tel: 344540, fax: 324173.

Beau Vallon and Surrounds:
There are three **main hotels** on Beau Vallon beach:
Beau Vallon Bay. Central location. 182 rooms, casino, pool, sports facilities; tel: 247141, fax: 247107.
Coral Strand. Central location. 103 rooms, watersports, pool, underwater dive centre; tel: 247517, fax: 247517.
Le Meridien Fisherman's Cove. 48 Rooms, elegant palm thatch, upmarket; tel: 247247, fax: 247742.

Some smaller ones are nearby:
Le Northolme. At Glacis. Secluded beach, French cuisine; tel: 261222, fax: 261223.
Sunset Beach. Glacis. Lovely sunsets over Silhouette; tel: 261111, fax: 261221.
Auberge Club Des Seychelles. 40 bungalows nestling amongst striking granite rocks and palms in the western corner of Bel Ombre; tel: 247550, fax: 247703.

GUEST HOUSES AND
BUDGET ACCOMMODATION
North Point Guest House. North Point. Chalets, self-catering facilities; tel: 241339, fax: 241850.
Manresa. Anse Etoile, 3km (2 miles) north of Victoria; tel: 241388.
Vacoa Village. Beau Vallon, self catering; tel: 261130, fax: 261146.
Carana Beach Chalets. North East Point. Upmarket, beachfront solitude; tel: 322642, fax: 225273.

North Mahé at a Glance

WHERE TO EAT

The small hotels, guest houses and restaurants all serve superb, gourmet cuisine on a par with any other country in the world.

There are at least 20 restaurants around Victoria and North Mahé. All are good, but none cheap by non-western price standards. Seafood and Kreol dishes are always specialities everywhere.

Four of the best restaurants in North Mahé are:

Auberge Louis XVII. French and Kreol cuisine on a *badamier* shaded verandah overlooking the harbour and inner islands. Good wines, good fish, excellent meat dishes; tel: 344411.

Restaurant Scala. Bel Ombre. Italian run, tasty shellfish; tel: 247535.

Le Corsaire. Right on the beach at Bel Ombre. Gracious atmosphere; tel: 247171.

Bagatelle. Sans Souci Road. New restaurant set in extensive tropical orchid gardens and bamboo forest up in the mountains; tel: 224722.

Others include:

Kyoto. Japanese, Anse Etoile; tel: 241337.

Etoile de Mer. Anse Etoile. Good continental and local cuisine; tel: 241327.

La Moutia. La Louise, tel: 344433.

King Wah. Chinese, Benezet Street, Victoria; tel: 323658.

La Perle Noire. Beau Vallon; tel: 247046.

Marie Antoinette. Grand Trianon, St Louis, above Victoria. Exotic old Seychelles house. Same menu for 16 years; tel: 266222.

Chez Gaby. Round Island, off Victoria. Excellent for lunches; tel: 322111.

Kapok Tree Restaurant. On lovely Cerf Island; tel: 322959.

Lobster Pot. Pointe Conan, north of Victoria, on waterfront; tel: 241376.

Cafe Moutia. Takeaways, Mont Fleuri; tel: 323363.

TOURS AND EXCURSIONS

There do not appear to be any real 'town tours' of Victoria, although Mason's, Travel Services Seychelles (TSS) and National Travel Agency (NTA) offer Mahé tours that include the market. Your own walking tour does just as well.

Victoria is the place to book all tours up the mountains, to the nearby islands, around Mahé, and so on.

Mason's Tours and Travel, tel: 322642, fax: 324173.

Travel Services Seychelles, tel: 322414, fax: 324010.

National Travel Agency, tel: 224900, fax: 225111.

Around Victoria:

Glass bottom boat for viewing coral reef, St Anne Marine Park. Contact Mason's Travel, tel: 322642, or their offices in major hotels.

Deep Sea Fishing. Several boats to choose from. Call in at Marine Charter in Victoria or tel: 322126.

Helicopter. Scenic trips around Mahé and to other islands. Helipads at airport and Victoria town, tel: 375400.

Scuba Diving. Try the Underwater Centre, Coral Strand Hotel, tel: 247357. Further down the beaches is Le Diable des Mers Diving Club, tel: 247104.

Island hopping. By air or sea. Contact any of the 3 major tour operators: Mason's, tel: 322642, NTA, tel: 224900, or TSS, tel: 322414.

Sailing, windsurfing. Contact The Manager, Seychelles Yacht Club, tel: 322362. They welcome temporary members.

USEFUL TELEPHONE NUMBERS

Tourist Information Office, Independence House, tel: 225313; and Airport, tel: 373136, fax: 224035.

Hertz, tel: 322447, fax: 324111.

Avis, tel: 224511.

Taxi, tel: 322279 (City) or 247499 (Beau Vallon).

Air Seychelles, tel: 225220, fax: 225159. (Domestic flights tel: 373101).

Marine Charter, tel: 322126.

Emergency: (Ask for ambulance, police or fire) tel: 999.

Telephone Operator: tel: 100 (International operator 151); International Calls (STD): Dial 0 and then the country code.

Doctor, tel: 323866/ 321911.

Dentist, tel: 224400.

Pharmacy, tel: 225559.

3
South and West Mahé

The southern and western areas of Mahé, caressed by the trade winds, are separated from Victoria and the main tourist areas by the island's central range of mountains. It was the last area to receive tarred roads, electricity, and larger hotels, and with a myriad hidden coves, coconut plantations and empty beaches, it is also the most rural and loveliest part of Mahé. Here you will find lone fishermen coming ashore to sell their catch of *karang* on the beach, deserted picnic coves, old plantation houses sleeping among the zak fruit and banana trees, people walking barefoot in the tiny villages, and old men on their way to the local store carrying palm frond shopping bags. As always the high, jungle-covered mountains brood above, offering cool, airy walks with wide views of hillside, reef and sparkling sea, while in the forests of Morne Seychellois National Park survives a living museum of unique and unusual plants and animals.

CENTRAL MAHÉ AND THE MOUNTAINS

The mountains of Mahé fall down to the sea in a riot of tropical greenery and dramatic black precipices. Rising abruptly out of the ocean, the mountains are almost constantly shrouded in swirling mist and flecked by bright sunlight, creating the dappled, eerie atmosphere of true montane forest, the hidden home of rare and exotic plants.

Morne Seychellois National Park covers 30km² (11 sq miles), incorporating the highest of Mahé's misty peaks and a large section of the western end of the island. The highest point is the mountain **Morne**

CLIMATE

The climate of south and west Mahé is really no different to the north. The southeasterly **trade winds** buffet the south coast, adding to the lonely wildness of some of the coves. With mist swirling around, there is much more chance of it **raining** up in the mountains than elsewhere, and if walking, you should be prepared for showers.

Opposite: *An avenue of sandragon trees, leading to the mountain viewpoint at Mission.*

Seychellois itself, at 905m (2970ft). There are no settlements and only one road through the park; it is all mountainous jungle, towering trees, and mysterious nature. From Victoria the **Sans Souci** mountain road over to Port Glaud cuts through the park, winding up the hillside and offering stunning views over the harbour and multi-pastel reef platforms below. It passes a number of interesting buildings, such as the American Embassy in a house called '1776', where Archbishop Makarios of Cyprus lived during his exile. As the often precipitous road twists its way under the towering peaks, it passes the starting points for signposted walking trails which lead into the park and up to the peaks of **Trois Frères**, **Copolia**, and **Morne Blanc** respectively. At **Mission** there is a platform with spectacular views over the western coast, while on the descent into Port Glaud the **Tea Tavern** is a good place to sample and buy tea gathered from the nearby estates.

Morne Seychellois National Park

The Park contains the best of the remaining indigenous forest of Seychelles, the giant lowland trees having been cut long ago, mainly to fuel cinnamon factories. There is something haunting and silently magnificent about the vast gothic cathedral of the forest. The canopy of trees soars 12m (40ft) above you as you walk, and all around green light plays on the **lichens, ferns,** straggling **creepers** and **old man's beard**. The best way to see the park beyond the road is to walk up one of the signposted paths. Other tracks are not well marked, and it is inadvisable to go too deeply into the unknown without a guide. Be careful of deep cracks between boulders which are often hidden by the carpet of damp leaves. Helpful leaflets for the three walking paths can be obtained from the Tourism Information Office in Victoria.

Nearly all of the 70 or so endemic flowering plants and trees of Seychelles are found somewhere in the National Park: **screwpines, palms,** *koko maron* (the coconut tree named after a runaway slave), **orchids** and the **pitcher plant**. It is highly likely that Morne Seychellois is home to the total world population of both the *bwa-d-fer* (ironwood), and the jellyfish tree, *bwa mediz*. This tree, which was sensationally rediscovered by botanists in 1970, is about 8m (26ft) high with tiny, rose-like flowers which become clusters of sunburnt fruit like upside-down parachutes, hence the name jellyfish. There are only about 50 of the trees growing, and are so rare that they merit their own genus.

Below left and right:
Kept moist by heavy rainfall and mist, the vegetation in the highest parts of the Mahé mountains is thick, green, mossy, and in many places gnarled with age.

Apart from the endemics, there are a lot of what botanists call exotics, not because they are spectacularly colourful, but because they are strangers. One example is the pale, grey-trunked **albizia** tree, which is common in Africa; another is the **cinnamon** bush, which has a sweet, pleasant smell if you crumple it in your hand.

Frogs such as the **pygmy piping frog**, which makes a lot of noise considering that it is only the size of a cowrie shell, are found in the wet uplands, and seven of Seychelles unique birds make use of the high green canopy. You might spot the **Seychelles kestrel**, or **bare-legged scops owl**, and you will see many long-tailed tropic birds planing in the winds.

Grand'Anse

Grand'Anse, on the west coast over the La Misère road, is a long curve of wave-lashed beach which is often completely deserted; in some ways it is even more attractive than Beau Vallon. Watched over by giant takamaka trees its waters lie open to the wind and ocean without the barrier of reef common to many of Mahé's beaches. The dangerous ocean currents running off the beach claimed the life of Governor John Thorp in 1961 as he was trying to rescue a child. In the southeast trade winds it is Seychelles' surfing beach.

Below: *From Mission in Morne Seychellois National Park, the wide views encompass the thick, tumbling landscape of southern Mahé.*

Mahé's soils are porous and low in fertility There are less than 1000ha (2500 acres) of arable land in Seychelles, and the country has to import much of its food requirements. The **Ministry of Agriculture Research Station** farm at Grand'Anse specialises in researching pawpaw, mango and a wide range of tropical fruits, with a

view to increasing their yield on the islands. Behind the strip of fertile land the mountains rise steeply into the Morne Seychellois National Park. This particular area is known as Grand Bois, which is believed to be a good place to find the elusive jellyfish tree, although you would need a guide to do so.

The aerials at the T-junction of the coastal road with the **La Misère** road belong to the BBC World Service Relay Station. If you head west here you pass Grand'Anse and reach **Port Glaud** and the **Sans Souci** road. Beyond this on the coast are the Marine National Parks at **Port Launay** and **Baie Ternay**, where hawksbill

Above: *Thérèse and Conception Islands from above Port Glaud.*
Below: *A green gecko on the husk of a sweet coconut.*

BEACHCOMBER

Seychelles attracts artists and eccentrics, but it is not a new phenomenon. One old dragoon officer was exiled to the islands by Napoleon, and was described thus: 'In appearance he was about fifty years of age, clothed in vestments of blue dungaree... his humble mansion was formed by a row of bamboos fixed in the ground and connected here and there by wicker-work: the roof was scantily thatched... it had a cane couch, converted at night into a bed, two rudely-shaped chairs, a ladder to ascend to a species of upper apartment formed only of loose planks. "Tis all" said he, with a smile, "my friends in France have left me; but it is enough – I am content"'.

Above: *The beautiful pink-throated vanilla orchid. It is unique to Seychelles.*

ORCHIDS

Worldwide there are 17,000 species of orchid. Seychelles is home to 25, most of them epiphitic, meaning that they grow on other plants.
• Wild *payanke* or tropic bird orchid, the national flower.
• Wild vanilla orchid: large white flowers with an orange peach centre that bloom after rain and die by noon. There is no vanilla in them.
• Orchid tree: pink and mauve flowers. The seeds of some varietals are sometimes used for coffee.
• Phaius, or ground forest orchid, with leaves over 30cm (1ft) in length.
• Cultivated vanilla: pale green flowers and thick leaves on vines zigzagging up stakes. Big business in Seychelles 100 years ago, deforested slopes are witness to its popularity. Today it largely grows wild on trees.

turtles breed, and the green-backed heron, or *makak* in Kreol, is often spotted. Port Launay is the site of the Seychelles National Youth Service training camp and is out of bounds.

Standing off the coast at this point are the two substantial islands of **Thérèse** and **Conception.** The latter has no beach but Thérèse is popular with picnickers from the Mahé Beach Hotel, which had no beach and had to make one from scratch. In front of Thérèse, the tiny **L'Islette** is a delightful spot sitting in the middle of the cove where the Mare aux Cochons river emerges. A variety of freelance water taxis, whose owners, it would seem, take some trouble to look like buccaneers, wait to take you the few hundred metres to L'Islette restaurant on the tiny island.

Barbarons

Barbarons is a low-lying plateau south of Grand'Anse which rises gradually from the coast through lush coconut plantations to a height of 600m (1970ft). Reef and rock lie close inshore with a wild and beautiful beach in front of the luxurious **Meridien Barbarons Hotel**; a little further down the **Chateau d'Eau** is a delightfully elegant and very French plantation house and small hotel.

An **orchid farm** run by the Seychelles Marketing Board is nearby. Orchids grow well in Seychelles and there are at least 25 local varieties, many of which are endemic. The farm is open to visitors.

THE SOUTH

Hidden coves with steep, bumpy dirt roads leading to them are a feature of South Mahé, and there always seems to be a charming little village behind these hidden gems. Some of the beaches are less than 50m (55yds) long and usually backed by heavy stands of takamaka trees leaning over the waters. It is in the south that the last *moutias* were danced, *casier* fishing traps lean up against trees, spoken English is more unusual, and domino players will gather in noisy groups in the villages. To this day folk from Anse Soleil or Quatre Bornes are regarded by the sophisticates of Victoria as coming from the sticks.

Anse Boileau

For many years it was thought that Lazare Picault, the first Frenchman to land in Seychelles, had done so in the bay named after him in South Mahé where the islands' largest hotel, the Plantation Club, is now sited. In fact he came ashore in the much more practical – for both anchoring sailing ship and beach-bound longboat – Boileau Bay, slightly further north. An ancient anchor above the beach serves as a memorial of his arrival.

A drive along the length of the bay leads past spindly coconut trees to the handsome church of **Notre Dame de Sept Douleurs** (Our Lady of Seven Sorrows), which has some magnificent hardwood marquetry covering both the high ceiling and its support columns in mottled, chevron zigzag patterns. The church is also the home of popular 'popsinger' priest **Gustave Lafortune**. He has recorded a cassette of songs in Kreol, titled 'For a better

MOUNTAIN ROADS

The roads over Mahé's mountains are steep and winding, offering wonderful views down both sides of the island. The three main passes are:

• **Sans Souci**: the road from Victoria through Morne Seychellois National Park. Goes past a number of paths, as well as Mission viewpoint and the Tea Tavern.

• **La Misère**: from just south of Victoria to Grand'Anse. Passes underneath the huge golfballs of the United States Tracking Station.

• **Montagne Posée**: between Ans aux Pins beach and Anse Boileau. Passes the Cable and Wireless Relay Station and goes though an area called Bon Espoir, or Good Hope.

Below: *Thérèse Island, a popular lunch spot facing Port Glaud.*

Above: *Peaceful calm at Anse Boileau.*

Seychelles'. The music, which includes cuts from the well-known groups Bwa Gayak and Jack Yokowo, is gently evocative. Sunday morning services are well worth listening in on.

From the beach the green coastal mountains stretch left and right like enveloping bird wings, in a vast panorama that prompted Picault to name Mahé the 'Isle of Abundance'. Part of the forest by the **Montagne Posée** mountain road that leads from Anse Boileau over to Anse aux Pines is still known as L'Abondance. There is a trail which starts by the Cable and Wireless Station near **Bon Espoir** at the top of the pass and leads to a summit of 501m (1645ft).

Corsair Country

Travelling further south along the coast road, you come to a rise above the road in the hook of **Anse la Mouche**, where there is a magnificent panorama of the whole of west Mahé – a great long tumble of mountain, cloud and sea. Other than the lofty perch of Mission in the hills there is probably no grander view on Mahé. Perhaps it is the reason why the Hodoul family settled in this area generations ago.

Mention the name of sea captain **Jean François Hodoul** to an old Seychellois and you'll probably notice a faint shiver. A pirate and successful privateer, 'Le Corsair' was also a man of refined and refined tastes, reputed to have the best table in Seychelles. A local almanac of 1819 records that Hodoul '... ravaged the Red Sea, Gulf of Persia, Malabar and Coromandel Coasts, Sumatra and Java', yet Seychelles was always his base and he settled down to run his estates – initially in Silhouette, then Beau

Vallon, before moving to Mamelles, just south of Victoria, where his great mansion still stands.

His descendants feature regularly in the history of the islands and in modern-day politics. The family house at Anse la Mouche is near 'La Residence' holiday villas, which are run by Marie-Anne Hodoul, the quiet, dark haired great-granddaughter of the pirate.

This area of the south coast has a number of old Seychelles plantation houses dotted along it. These venerable gems, with their coral raised verandas, rusty tin roofs and big wooden exteriors, are usually hidden back from the beach among flowers and thick greenery. If you are not a beach person, wander from cove to cove house

Above: *The tangle of the tropics at Anse la Mouche.*
Below: *Baie Lazare, deserted and still.*

Above: *The old plantation house between Takamaka and Quatre Bornes, one of the very few which still boasts a palm-thatched roof.*
Opposite: *Evening shadows and thoughtful glances are cast across a boat-yard game of dominoes.*

ARTISTS' STUDIOS

• Michael Adams, in an old colonial house at Anse aux Poules Bleues.
• Italian painter Antonio Filippin at the Yellow Gallery at Beau Vallon.
• Tom Bowyers, sculptor, is at Santa Maria, Anse la Mouche.
• Vladimir Tarakanoff's studio is near Le Northolme Hotel, at Glacis.
• Jeanne D'Offay, a painter of landscapes, is at Le Cap.

hunting, as wherever there's an open and flat piece of land there's usually an old residence. One of the charms of Seychelles is that almost every old home is a museum in its own right, with a treasure trove of little historical artifacts. British civil servants were fond of denigrating the planters, but in an agriculturally hostile environment it was always a struggle to introduce and sustain new crops, plants and animals. They did, however, have pawpaws, coconuts, breadfruit, spices, tamarinds and their stern God to sustain them. And the sort of views you get at Anse la Mouche.

The Southern Tip

As the road turns out of Anse la Mouche over to **Baie Lazare**, you will find the studio of famous Seychelles artist Michael Adams overlooking **Anse aux Poules Bleues**. A little further on there is a broken road which leads to **Anse Soleil's** tiny, sunset-shimmering beach. There is an old sugar cane mill in the forest which fringes the beach, possibly the only one left in Seychelles.

After Baie Lazare on the road from **Takamaka** (named after the huge tree prevalent on the beach), a handsome 100 year-old palm-thatched plantation house stands among a garden of tropical flowers. It is possibly the only thatched roof of its kind in Seychelles, the rest having adopted corrugated iron decades ago.

After the road turns from the western coastline, it comes to **Quatre Bornes**, a rather attractive little crossroads village of brightly-coloured shops hanging over the road and valley. Visit any of these little southern villages on a Sunday and you'll see the scenes of old-fashioned, rural Mahé: football games in the dusty road, quartets of hand slapping domino players beneath the mango trees, and all the homes perched on the hillside, with neat gardens and neighbours sitting chatting by their front porch.

From Quatre Bornes a road leads to a series of nine coves and the southern tip of the island, **Cap Malheureux**. It is a windswept area of twisting hills and an ever-widening seascape. Not all the roads are suited for two-wheel-drive cars, and show discretion swimming at the small, lonely bays which, with no reefs to negotiate, may have been ideal for pirate longboats, but they are not protected from the shifting currents that sweep around this wild coast, land's end of Mahé.

Jardin du Roi

200 years ago, **Pierre Poivre**, administrator of the Ile de France (the name at that time for Mauritius), sponsored an expedition to Seychelles to set up a spice nursery. He believed that conditions in Mahé might allow the crops to compete with those fabulous spices of the east that the Dutch had monopolised for so long.

The spot chosen for the garden was on a broad, low-lying plain of rich black soil well watered by two rivers, just up from the longest beach on the island, called **Anse Royale**, in the southeast of Mahé. The nursery developed gradually, first rivalling the earlier, private venture at the settlement on St Anne's Island, and eventually replacing it. Within eight years they had cultivated cloves, nutmeg, and pepper brought in from the Moluccas in Indonesia, and cinnamon from Ceylon. The nursery was deliberately burnt to the ground in 1780 when the farmers were told a British ship was sailing into Port Royale (Victoria)

CINNAMON

You will find cinnamon growing wild all over Seychelles. The spice was introduced at the Jardin du Roi on Mahé in 1772 and, of all the spice trees, has proved to be the most successful in Seychelles. Although not of major economic importance today, 25 years ago it provided 30% of Seychelles foreign currency exports, while copra and cinnamon accounted for 90% of visible domestic exports. The flavour comes from the bark of the tree and is still sold in the form of rolls or quills to visitors.

harbour, as the secrets of the spices were too valuable to fall into the enemy's hands. The man o'war turned out to be French.

In 1994 three young Seychellois of French descent and with a sense of history opened their own Jardin du Roi at Anse Royale. **Alain St Ange**, **Bernard Georges** and **Jean François Ferrari's** garden of 40ha (100 acres) is planted not only with the original spices, but such modern additions as cardamom and the 19th-century money spinner patchouli. It is a great spot to wander among the scented trees and flowers. There is a cinnamon distillery in the grounds, evocative of the times when there was one in every bay on Mahé, the pungent brown water running onto and staining the beach, as well as a museum and reptile house. A creperie serves plantation fruit punches. From the hill above the garden, Roche Gratte Fesse (literally 'scratch your bum rock'), there are splendid views of Anse Royale's beach, village and the towers of the two churches built right on the beach, one Anglican, and the other Catholic.

Anse aux Pins

Just around the corner from the airport, Anse aux Pins is a substantial little village with a gorgeous sweep of close reef stretching from the village to the casuarina-tufted **Pointe au Sel**, 6km (3.5 miles) distant. The rumble of the breakers can be heard night and day, as the thin, pine-like filao that give the beach its name fret in the trades, although the trees aren't in fact true pines at all.

WALKS

Trail pamphlets are available from the Tourism Information office in Victoria, and Mason's Travel offers walking tours. There are seven walks, all marked with paint spots and wooden posts:

• **No 5. Trois Frères**. In Morne Seychellois National Park, a trail to the top of Trois Frères (699m; 2293ft), the second highest mountain on the island. Start near Sans Souci Forestry Station. Spectacular views, but beware of cloud and do not stray from path. 4 – 5 hours.

• **No 6**. Tea Factory to **Morne Blanc** (667m; 2188ft). Lovely west coast views. The Morne Blanc cliff face drops straight down 250m (820ft). 4 – 5 hours.

• **Copolia**. On eastern side of Sans Souci road, past the forest station. Up to a height of 497m (1630ft). 3 hours.

• There are other walks to the summit of **Mt Brulée** between Anse Boileau and Anse aux Pins, from Bel Ombre beach to **Anse Major**, and around **Victoria**.

Right: *The colonial house at the Craft Village near Anse aux Pins.*

ON THE MOVE

There are 250km (155 miles) of tarred roads on Mahé, some 5500 passenger cars, 1700 commercial vehicles and 150 motorcycles. Indian *Tata* buses are the main form of public transport, though minibuses are becoming popular. The days of rickshaws have recently passed, while heavy, flat-bottomed pirogue canoes were once the fastest way to go anywhere. Manned by 12 oarsmen, they would power along to a gentle sound of singing. Now the waters are graced by the large, inter-island schooners.

Being so close to the airport, this bay is often the last view visitors have of Seychelles, as their jet gains altitude above the emerald sea. Anse aux Pines is the site of Seychelles' first big holiday hotel, the **Reef**. Saturday night dances there are still popular, along with its famous poolside fish barbecues. There is a golf course (nine-hole) here, the only one for a radius of 1600km (1000 miles).

The **Kreol Institute** for furthering the language and culture of Seychelles is housed in an old plantation house called Maison St Joseph halfway down the bay. Next to it is the **Codevar** craft village and **La Marine**, an old Kreol house where Seychelles hardwoods are carved and replicas of old sailing boats skillfully assembled. The beach is not the best as the reef is too close – although it can be good for finding octopus.

Above: *The main road winding past Anse Royale.*
Below: *Model ships, carefully and expertly built at La Marine.*

South and West Mahé at a Glance

For further information see also North Mahé at a Glance (pp54 - 55)

BEST TIMES TO VISIT

It rains heavily in **December**, **January** and **February**, while the southeast tradewinds from **April** to **October** bring refreshing breezes to all but the northwest of the island. The temperature stays at a steady 27°C (81°F) throughout the year, with a tropical humidity of 80-85%. Many hotels have air conditioning; others, cool fans and large shuttered windows.

GETTING THERE

Other than cruise ships or your own yacht, the only way to get to Mahé is to **fly**. There are scheduled services from Africa (Johannesburg and Nairobi), Europe, and the Middle and Far East. The international airport is on the east coast of Mahé, 15 minutes drive from Victoria. Airport **transfers** are usually organized by hotels or tour operators.

GETTING AROUND

Car hire, usually an open mini moke, is the favourite vehicle for touring the rural areas of Mahé. There are practically no gravel roads left, and plenty of passes over the mountains. These are steep, winding roads with marvellous views of forest and shore far below. Beware of steep drops off the narrow roads and tight corners. The speed limit is 65kph (40mph in

town and villages). There are not many petrol stations and hire cars do not come with a full tank. **Bicycles and motorbikes** can also be hired from various outlets. **Taxis** are available in Victoria, the airport, and at the larger hotels. 24 hour service. Note that taxi fares are relatively expensive.

One of the best ways to get around is on the local **minibuses**. The service is pretty regular and inexpensive, but they don't operate after 18:30. The **regular bus service** is available around the beaches and villages of South Mahé and over the mountains. Call out *'devan'* ('up ahead') when you want to disembark.

WHERE TO STAY

The large package tour holiday hotels are sited on the best beaches. They include:
Mahé Beach Hotel. Near Port Glaud, elevated position; tel: 378451.
Equator Sun. West coast near Grand'Anse. Lovely sea view, lovely pool; tel: 378228, fax: 378244/378402.
Le Meridien Barbarons. West coast near Barbarons Estate. Nice palms and scenic walks; tel: 378253, fax: 378484/ 378327.
Plantation Club. Southwest coast, Val Mer. 200 rooms, casino, dive centre; tel: 361361, fax: 361333.

Reef Golf Club Hotel. Anse aux Pins. With golf course, near airport; tel: 376251, fax: 376296.

SMALL HOTELS AND BUDGET

NB. All family run establishments will trade on prices. Book for a shorter time and then see what is on offer. In Seychelles generally, the smaller the hotel, the better it tends to be.
L'Islette. Port Glaud. Four rooms on a tiny offshore island. Popular weekend restaurant venue; tel: 378229, fax: 378499.
Chateau d'Eau. Barbarons. Colonial Plantation House, five rooms; tel: 378577, fax: 378388.
La Residence. Anse la Mouche. Seven spacious self-catering villas and duplex flats; tel: 322682/ 371370, fax: 321322.
Carefree Guest House. Anse aux Pins, very near airport. Four rooms, good value; tel: 375237.
Hotel Allamanda. Anse Forbans, south coast. Small hotel, right on the beach. 10 rooms; tel: 371334, fax: 371675.
Auberge de Bougainville. Bougainville, south coast. Old Plantation House with seven rooms in tropical gardens; tel: 371788, fax: 371808.
Hotel Casuarina. Southeast coast, lovely trees, 15 rooms; tel: 376211.

South and West Mahé at a Glance

For further information see also North Mahé at a Glance (pp54 -55)

WHERE TO EAT

Every guest house and hotel has a restaurant and all usually accept drop-by diners. Restaurants in the large hotels are seldom as good as the smaller, family-run establishments. Try:

Au Capitaine Rouge. Oscar Restaurant, Anse la Mouche. Provençal dishes; tel: 371224.

Kaz Kreol. Anse Royale. Bit of everything, good atmosphere; tel: 371680.

Pomme Cannelle. Inside crafts village at Anse Aux Pins. Recommended for tasting almost forgotten Kreol dishes. Try the fruit bat in wine; tel: 376155.

Jolie Rose. Anse Intendance, south Mahé; tel: 371170.

Ty Foo. Le Cap, east coast. Chinese and Kreol food among palms, facing beach; tel: 371485.

La Palafitte. Grand'Anse, west coast, in Equator Sun Hotel. Great seaviews; tel: 378228.

Sundown. Port Glaud, west coast. In small seafront rural village; tel: 378352.

La Sirene. Anse aux Poules Bleues; see Michael Adams studio nearby; tel: 361339.

Katiolo Night Club. Anse Faure, southeast coast. In an old boatshed near airport. tel: 375453.

Tec Tec Lodge. Anse Louis on south coast. In a small guest house, so ring first; tel: 376430.

TOURS AND EXCURSIONS

Bird watching. Contact Adrian Skerrett, tel: 322100. For information read any books by him, or Ian Bullock's *Birds of the Republic of Seychelles*.

Golf. Reef Hotel Golf Club, tel: 376251.

Walking trails. Morne Seychellois National Park etc. Contact Mason's Travel, tel: 322642, who can arrange a guide. Trail maps available from Tourist Office in Victoria.

Diving. Any large hotel will advise on local outfits.

Dancing. The larger hotels feature sega music and dancing displays, usually at weekends. Check with Tourist Information for any special town concerts.

Tennis. Available at most large hotels.

Fishing. Marine Charter in Victoria; tel: 322126. Many fishermen operate from coastal bays and beaches, and will sometimes take you along on their smaller boat. There is an **inter-island helicopter service**, Helicopter Seychelles, with a helipad in

Victoria, tel: 375400. Also **Helicopter scenic trips** around Mahé and to other islands. Helipads at airport and in Victoria.

Reef exploring. Wear a pair of tough shoes and wade or swim to the reef at low tide. Or go by boat. Don't snorkel alone, never collect live shells or coral, and be wary of spiky black sea urchins.

Casino. At the Plantation Club, Baie Lazare.

USEFUL TELEPHONE NUMBERS

Tourist Information Office, Independence House, Victoria, tel: 225313 or 373136 (Seychelles Airport).

Car hire. Hertz, tel: 322447. Avis, tel: 224511. Many more.

Bicycle hire. Try North Bicycle Rental, tel 247036.

Taxis. Anse aux Pins, tel: 375609; Barbarons, tel: 378629.

National Parks, tel: 224644.

Maps purchase, tel: 224030.

Doctor, tel: 321911 or 323866 (both in Victoria).

Dentist, tel: 224400.

Emergency, tel: 999.

Phone operator, tel: 100.

GRAND ANSE	J	F	M	A	M	J	J	A	S	O	N	D
AVERAGE TEMP. °F	81	82	82	82	82	81	79	79	79	81	81	79
AVERAGE TEMP. °C	27	27.5	28	28	28	27	26	26	26.5	27	27	26.5
Hours of Sun Daily	5	6	7	8	8	8	8	7	7	8	7	6
SEA TEMP. °F	82	80	82	80	78	77	73	73	73	79	77	80
SEA TEMP. °C	28	27	28	27	26	25	23	23	23	26	25	27
RAINFALL in	17	7	25	7	9	6	5	7	7	9	9	11
RAINFALL mm	422	180	237	175	233	146	130	170	169	225	233	274
Days of Rainfall	11	6	7	6	8	6	6	6	7	6	8	10

4
Praslin

For many people, the island of Praslin is the real Seychelles. A rural, languid island of beaches, palms, and country roads, it has all the ingredients of the Garden of Eden image that made Seychelles famous. High in the hills, the **Vallée de Mai** is home to the 100 foot-tall coco de mer palms, that bear the largest fruit in the world. Theories have suggested that the giant palms are the biblical trees of Adam and Eve, and the valley the paradise that man was heir to before being tempted into mortality.

Sited 40km (25 miles) east of Mahé, Praslin is the archipelago's second largest island, 11km (7 miles) long and 4km (2.5 miles) wide. It is the choice holiday spot of Seychellois themselves, and visitors who have discovered it tend not to linger too long at Mahé airport as they transfer to one of the small Otter aircraft that make the 15 minute hop across the ocean.

Praslin's highest peak, at 367m (1204ft), is only a third that of Morne Seychellois on Mahé, and its population is less than 7000 people. There are no towns, and only two villages at **Grand'Anse** and **Baie Ste Anne**, where the old-fashioned schooners tie up. But even in these quaint settlements you never get the impression of there being many people around, for Praslin is laid back, relaxed, and unspoilt in every way. The pace of life encourages you to explore on foot, to a distant beach, up the trails in the hills, or simply along to a lone corner shop on the Anse Kerlan road. You may well meet one of the eccentric and interesting artists, writers and bohemians the island seems to attract, and come to understand the

Opposite: *The diamond-pure sands of Anse Lazio, in northwest Praslin.*

DON'T MISS

*** Vallée de Mai, home of the coco de mer fruit and palms. World Heritage Site. Trails and curio shop.
*** A visit to Café des Arts. Paintings and crafts by Seychelles artists on beautiful Côte d'Or beach.
** Bicycle ride around the mainly flat circular road from Côte d'Or to Baie Ste Anne, Consolation, Grand'Anse and Anse Kerlan.
** Dive or snorkel in the Marine Park in Curieuse Bay.
* Explore Grand'Anse Village and Baie Ste Anne.
* Walk to Anse Volbert or Baie Chevalier.

depth of affection in an old island song. 'Praslin, mon Praslin,' it goes, 'I will never let you go'.

The economy of Praslin was founded for many years on coconut, vanilla, and patchouli plantations, fishing and quarrying (Praslin's red granite is prized for building facades on Mahé), but increasingly the island has set its foundations in tourism. However, refreshingly sensitive to the dangers of overplaying their hand, the government has set a ceiling of 950 hotel beds on the island, so it is unlikely that the casual charm of Praslin will be lost.

AROUND PRASLIN

Grand'Anse

Grand'Anse is and always has been the bohemian backwater of Seychelles. It is on the western side of Praslin, but remains exposed to the trade winds that come thrashing through the palms, with waves tearing endlessly at the long line of reef far out to sea. The first hotel on Praslin, a thatched two-roomed bungalow used by the visiting Mahé doctor on his rounds of the islands, is still there after 40 years, though now refurbished and part of a lovely series of chalets on the beach called Indian Ocean Lodge. In the early days it was given the glamourous name of Mickey Mouse – and one of the guests over the years was another Hollywood star called Ronald Reagan.

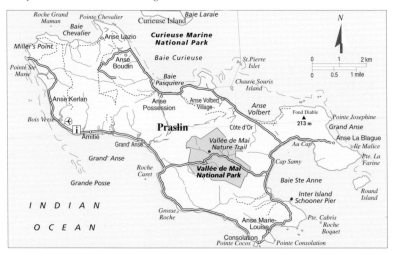

ST MATTHEW APOSTLE CHURCH

Built in the 1850s, the Grand'Anse church is one of four Anglican churches in Seychelles. It incorporates a large white cross on the beach, which is used as a guide by passing fishermen. The interior is a sky-blue with giraffe spots, and there is a notice which says, 'I am a happy Anglican, do not disturb my faith.'

With a number of **hotels** and **restaurants,** such as the venerable Flying Dutchman with its ship's navigation lights and bottle of rum ambience, Grand'Anse is the social hub of the island. The village almost seems to be deliberately cultivating a ramshackle image, as apart from the smart Barclays Bank and Luc's Super Store, most of the colourfully painted tin-roofed buildings look like they might fall over at any moment. There's a fish market, a plantation house, a tiny library and post office, and Mr Pillay, 'dealer in tobacco spirits and wines'. Peaking over the palms is the steeple of **St Matthew the Apostle,** a church dedicated in 1859. The locals hang out at Ivey's Bar, with its video and football machines, while the coco de mer-crested independence monument is a favourite place to stop, chat and have a beer.

Grand'Anse is not a good swimming beach by Seychelles' superlative standards, but the seaweed-strewn sand is a favourite with beachcombers. Between the sea and the hills a wide plain with coconut trees wafts back from the narrow road that hides the occasional house and the handsome bell tower of **St Joseph's** church.

Baie Ste Anne

Behind Grand'Anse stands the central ridge of Praslin's hills with their distinctive patches of red granite soil. The mountains were once covered in huge forests but

---

BOHEMIA-ON-SEA

Praslin has always been a magnet for writers, poets, artists and plain old-fashioned eccentrics who have dropped out into Eden. You have to winkle them out of their small tin and brightly coloured houses set among the spindly palms and up the steep breadfruit-shaded tracks that lead into the hills, but they tend to come down of their own accord to coastal watering holes like Brittania Confait's and the Flying Dutchman as evening falls, to watch the sky turn pastel pink and blue across reef and ocean, then die in a rage of fire through the palms.

Above: *The inter-island ferry,* La Belle Praslinoise, *alongside the jetty at Baie Ste Anne.*

sadly fire ravaged them long ago. The main road climbs through the hills, passing the entrance to the Vallée de Mai near the summit, before descending towards the wide curve of Baie Ste Anne.

Baie Ste Anne is the capital of Praslin, if such an expression can be justified by this sleepy seaside village with its little cluster of small shops, school, hospital, and power plant. On the beachfront you might still see men climbing the coconut trees to extract calou toddy. The spider scramble up the trees that young men used to perform is rare these days, so look out for the trees with ladders leaning against them.

The village has always been a wooden boat-building centre and is the landing stage for the inter-island schooners from Mahé and La Digue. The trip to Mahé takes about three hours, and there are usually two sailings daily. Arriving at Baie Ste Anne from the sea is always a lovely sight with the sweep of sparkling bay, fishing boats anchored, and the green rise up to the mysterious forest behind.

Côte d'Or

Côte d'Or, on the north of the island, is Praslin's finest beach, a 3km (2 mile) long stretch of soft white sand fringed with palms and lovely yellow sea hibiscus. These flowers have a deep purple centre which turns orange by afternoon. Côte d'Or has a string of hotels, including one with a casino, and holiday activities that include windsurfing, sailing, and diving and snorkelling trips to **Curieuse Island Marine Park**, which is close by at the western end of the bay. You can even explore the depths on a

---

GO LOCAL

A little Kreol goes a long way on Praslin. Here are some useful expressions (pronounce phonetically):

Where are we now?	*Kot nou ete la?*
Are you going to the Vallée de Mai?	*Ou pe al Vallée de Mai?*
Is this our boat for La Digue?	*Sa nou bato pour La Digue?*
Is Anse Kerlan far?	*I lwen Anse Kerlan?*
Can you play moutia?	*Ou konn zwe moutia?*
What is this beach called?	*Kimwanyer sa lans i apele?*
What is this fish called?	*Kimwanyer sa pwason i apele?*

night dive. There's a delightful little restaurant and hotel on what must be the smallest inhabited island in Seychelles, Chauve Souris (Fruit Bat Island), which stands a few hundred metres off the beach.

Hidden from the larger hotels is the **Café des Arts**, a beach restaurant, crafts centre, and art gallery located opposite Chauve Souris. Praslin is a perfect place for painters – full of empty country roads, relaxed villages, red hills, distant islands, and a deserted beach at the end of each winding track. A number of artists live on Praslin, and many more make it their holiday retreat. The Café des Arts is run by artist Christine Harter and Canadian photographer Paul Turcotte, and their gallery actively encourages every visual art in the islands. The Café is a popular meeting place, with its Parisian ambience and views out over the azure waters of the never ending ocean.

Towards the other end of Côte d'Or from Café des Arts is a large agricultural estate with palms, casuarina trees and browsing cattle. Set on stilts in one corner is the tiny house that once belonged to Henri Dauban (See Silhouette, p109) and who did so much experimenting with and development of farming techniques on this long, tree-filled flatland. A mangrove swamp survives in the corner, with crabs digging around in the cracked mud

---

PAINTER IN PARADISE

Marie Andre Christine de Lacoudraye Harter is possibly the finest artist in Seychelles. Certainly her evocative work captures the quiet relaxation of Praslin like no other. Graduating with an honours degree in fine art in the UK, she taught for many years. 10 years ago she moved from Mahé to Praslin and opened the Café des Arts restaurant and gallery with husband Paul Turcotte.

FRUIT BAT

The endemic flying fox or *chauve souris* looks like something out of Dracula, though close-up it resembles a little brown furry fox.

● Unlike other bats, the *chauve souris* (literally, it means skittermouse) sees very well.

● Unlike other bats, it eats no insects or meat at all, only fruit.

● It has a wing spread of 1m (3.5 ft).

● They cannot echo locate like other bats.

● Fruit bats play a major role in the reproduction of plants in Seychelles by disseminating fruit seeds.

● Fruit bat is eaten as a delicacy in Seychelles.

Left: *Chauve Souris Island, the charming location of a tiny hotel and restaurant.*

and small red, white and blue flowers on the sandy pathways. The small birds fluttering at your feet are the *toutrel coco* or barred ground dove, supposed to bring peace and good luck.

A long, isolated road goes past stands of passion fruit with their green, egg-shaped fruit and white tendril flowers, and reaches the elegant Archipel villas.

Above: *St Pierre Islet, on the edge of Curieuse Marine National Park.*

From here a path leads along the wild and rocky coast around **Devil's Peak**, or Fond Diable ('fond', a term which is used for most of the hills on Praslin, is an old French word meaning hat, or crown). This leads to another, lesser known, **Grande Anse,** which faces a coterie of lovely islands: Félicité, Petite Soeur, Grande Soeur, Ile Cocos and the larger island of La Digue.

Below left and right:
The massive double nut of the coco de mer: husked and in its shell.

VALLEE DE MAI

Though Praslin is generously blessed with stunning beaches and a wonderfully laid back atmosphere, the peculiar attraction of the island is to be found in a small

Left: *Deep inside the emerald-tinged Vallée de Mai forest.*

CONSERVATIONISTS

For many years, nature was considered boundless by the inhabitants of Seychelles. In 1769 Abbe Alexis Rochon was the first scientist to visit the islands, and in 1788 the first true conservationist arrived, the administrator Jean Baptiste Philogene de Malavois. He made recommendations for the protection of Seychelles' timber, tortoises and turtles, but sadly they were not heeded. In modern times, Seychellois such as Guy Lionnet and Kantilal Jivan Shah have done much to encourage interest in Seychelles' flora, fauna and history. With the coming of the airport Seychelles has received the assistance of western countries, conscious perhaps of the terrible destruction wreaked on their own wilderness resources.

---

area of thick forest high up in the green hills. Here the famous **coco de mer** tree has its last natural habitat, in a slumbering valley of giants known as the Vallée de Mai (though often abbreviated to Val de Mai). The Vallée, an area of only 18ha (45 acres) enclosed within Praslin National Park's larger 338ha (834 acres), is a World Heritage Site, one of only two in Seychelles.

The whole national park area was so remote and mountainous that it remained totally untouched until the 1930s – a saving grace for the indigenous trees. Trail leaflets lead you to some of these, including the *bwa rouz*, with leaves like corrugated cardboard, and *northea kapisen*, with its horizontal cracked-mud bark. The leaflets are available at the entrance to the reserve, from where the well laid out circular path begins. The car park, with a curio shop and tea garden close by, is about halfway along the mountain road between Grand'Anse and Baie Ste Anne.

52 of Seychelles' indigenous plants and trees can be seen in this extraordinary valley, including all six endemic palm species. It is the last habitat of the unique **black parrot**, of which there are perhaps less than 100 left. A few unusual reptiles are also found, including the bright green **Praslin gecko**, the non-poisonous **wolf snake**, the **tiger chameleon**, and a number of different **frogs**.

Right: *The long, flower-speckled catkin on a male coco de mer palm.*

The main attraction, however, is the coco de mer. As you walk into the forest, the silence is overwhelming. Above and close around are the phalanxes of monstrous palms, soaring 30m (100ft) to a sombre canopy of knife pleated fronds the width of a room, with clusters of nuts weighing 18kg (40lb) each. When a light breeze disturbs one of the slumbering trees, it fidgets and rasps its fronds against a neighbour, while a gust of wind coming up the valley from Baie Ste Anne will send the huge trees into a frenzy of clattering branches which sound like coconuts in a storm falling on a tin roof. Then, just as suddenly as it started, the unwieldy giants will rest again, reform-ing their eerie atmosphere of swirling, sunlight-pierced green light.

Ever since the coco de mer made its first, mysterious appearances around the fringes of the Indian Ocean, it has been the source of legend, wonder, and erotic delight. The nut which grows on the shorter female tree looks like a gigantic green acorn, but husked, the black, hard-shelled double coconut strikes a remarkable resemblance to a female's nether regions, while the 1m (3ft) long catkin, covered in yellow flowers, provides the male biological adjunct. Understandably believed to have aphrodisiacal and medicinal powers, the fabled nut commanded fortunes from princes and potentates around India and the

Middle East. Sailors knew the coco de mer palm as the tree that emerged from the ocean and provided a nest for the giant *rukh*, or roc, which has a 50m (150ft) wingspan and would carry off any unwary seamen who came too close. The Japanese considered the nut sacred, Indian princes fashioned them into jewelled drinking gourds, and one was even priced at 4000 golden florins.

Above: *30m above the ground, the nuts on a female coco de mer.*

It was not long before the coco de mer aroused interest in a totally different way. General (then Colonel) 'Chinese' Gordon visited Praslin in 1881 and wrote a lengthy dissertation entitled 'Eden and Its Two Sacramental Trees'. The breadfruit, he decided, was the Tree of Life, while the coco de mer was the Tree of Good and Evil. At a time when the theory of evolution was being hotly debated and Darwin excoriated, Gordon believed in a literal interpretation of the Bible. Step by step he explained the Book of Genesis in terms of Praslin, the Val de Mai and the coco de mer palm. It may not have found its way into mainstream theology but his theories were to become the pivotal drawcard of Seychelles tourism: the scented Garden of Eden, a tropical paradise among the palms, islands of love a thousand miles from anywhere in the far Indian Ocean. And few can deny the effectiveness of the image.

Praslin Island Walks

Praslin is small enough that cycling and walking are an excellent way to get to know the island. There is hardly any traffic on the island, it is relatively flat around much of the coastline, and there are plenty of quiet paths leading through old plantations and out to windswept viewpoints. Buses run regularly around the coastal road, so it is never difficult to get back to your hotel.

Anse Possession: Leaving from **St Matthew's Church** in Grand'Anse a path passes the attractive Brittania guest house and leads up into breadfruit tree plantations scattered with rock-perched houses. At the saddle in the mountain divide are two tin houses, one pink and one blue, which look out over the ocean to Mahé. From here the right-hand path heads towards the pretty beach at **Côte d'Or**, while the left-hand track follows the **Pasquière River** down to Anse Possession, site of Dufresne's first landing, and now part of **Curieuse Marine National Park**.

> **DUFRESNE**
>
> Chevalier Marion Dufresne, the man who claimed Praslin for France in 1768, was a man who had an eye for historic moments. Twelve years earlier he had picked up Bonnie Prince Charlie off the Scottish coast after the Young Pretender had been defeated by the English at Culloden. Dufresne is supposed to have buried a deed of claim at Anse Possession, and, needless to say, people have been trying to find it ever since.

Southern Tip: Another route is to go south out of Grand'Anse, carry on past the turning to Val de Mai, and walk along the coast road as waves crash against the sea wall at high tide, spray almost touching the palm fronds. There is a collection of pocket sized bays with

Right: *The coastal road on Praslin threads between thick vegetation and dazzling beach. Numerous wooden houses and tiny shacks are hidden in the abundant greenery.*

Left: *Ocean rollers dashing against chunky granite boulders, which lie strewn over the white sand at Baie Chevalier.*

names such as **Cemetery**, **Boat,** and **Consolation**, each one of them with highrise cliffs and crowding takamaka trees. **Coco Point** is the southern tip of Praslin; from here it is not too far over to **Baie Ste Anne**.

Baie Chevalier: One of the most pleasant walks (especially early in the morning) is to go north to Baie Chevalier. From Grand'Anse you walk past the airstrip at **Amitié**, where the road becomes concrete (a lapse in aesthetic focus, but helpful as the odd tide washes over it). **Cousin** and **Cousine** islands, the enchanting siblings of North Praslin, are 2km (1.2 miles) off the almost blinding snow-white beach. At the end of the road you reach a rocky viewpoint jutting out to sea called **Pointe Ste Marie**. It overlooks **Anse Kerlan** and the south coast, and in the other direction the even prettier **Petite Anse Kerlan**, tucked in the lea of the little headland. A white handmade concrete cross stands on the point in memory of a child who drowned here many years ago.

Doubling back a short way, a path then leads over the red earth hills covered in latanier palms and pandanus until it reaches the deep blue water and white curve of sand at Baie Chevalier, the quintessential tropical bay. The

---

CREEPY CRAWLIES AND OTHER HAZARDS

- There are no poisonous snakes in Seychelles.
- Scorpions and centipedes are rare, but scratchy sand-flies are felt on the beaches.
- Beware of sunburn. Use factor 15+ cream.
- Treat coral scratches with an antiseptic.
- See a doctor if you get earache or infection from swimming in coral waters.
- There *is* AIDS in Seychelles.
- Don't sit or sunbathe under coconut trees.

Above: *A schooner lying off Anse Lazio beach.*

SPICE ISLANDS

The first French settlers came to the islands to plant spices. Only cinnamon really survived, but the islands have been spicy ever since:
- Lemon grass, or *sitronel*. Long tufted green grass, lovely as a tea.
- Cinnamon, or *kanel*. Leaves look like spear tips, and are used with bark for cinnamon oil and in cooking. Used to be a major plantation industry, and still found everywhere.
- Patchouli. Its dried scented leaves were used instead of moth balls, and its oil is a fixative in perfume.
- Cloves. The prized spice of pomanders and chefs that countries went to war over.
- Plus nutmegs, vanilla, ginger, chillies, pepper and all the spice of life.

---

bay, deep and reef free, is a popular yacht anchorage, and now also boasts a good restaurant revelling in the name of Bonbon Plume. From the restaurant a road leads to **Anse Boudin**, where the round-Praslin buses start up again.

CURIEUSE

Curieuse Island, not much more than a kilometre off the northern coast of Praslin, lies completely within the boundaries of Curieuse Marine National Park. The area is home to both fish and coral of every extraordinary variety and colour; snorkelling or diving in the clear, warm water is a chance to feast on the silent wonder of the living reef.

The garden under the sea is every bit as exotic as that on the islands behind. Rounded brain corals, stag corals, spiky black sea urchins, giant cowries, purple-lipped clams, and thousands of darting, flashing fish can all be seen. There are blushing brown octopus, sharp-toothed barracuda, moray eels darting from their caverns with a warning glower, batfish, lovely blue and yellow surgeon fish, big horned and drowsy Picasso trigger fish, grouper, angelfish and the elegant needle-thin trumpet fish. Loveliest of all is the dappled brown hawksbill turtle, winging away in the blue. Some 40 hawksbill – a species unfortunately still much sought after to make tortoise-shell ornaments and jewellery – crawl up onto the beautiful white beach facing Praslin each year to lay their eggs. There should be many more: the park contains a large, abandoned, turtle pond at **Baie Larai**, which was built 80 years ago and can be crossed by a 500m (550 yd) long causeway running across the mouth of the bay.

The island, 3.5km (2 miles) long, is the home to giant land tortoises and a tortoise conservatory, coco de mer palms and black parrots, but they are all borrowed from Aldabra and Praslin. The trail on the island is excellent, with tagged and numbered trees that include the indigenous *calice du pape*, screwpine, *bwa rouz* and many others.

Curieuse, which is easily reached by boat from the Côte d'Or resorts, is not as protected as the slightly more distant islands of Cousin and Aride. Originally called Ile Rouge because of its distinctive red soils, it was a leper colony for 50 years during the 19th century. The ruins of the village can still be seen, as well as the old Kreol house built by a Scottish doctor in 1873. Curieuse's vast stands of towering hardwood trees were cleared to plant coconuts at the turn of the century, but under the protection provided by the National Park, a reforestation scheme has been implemented.

PRASLIN FEAST

A special Seychelles menu to get your mouth watering:

Stuffed *palourde* clams

•

Tectec soup with a drop of island rum

•

Coetivy crayfish with *citrons*

•

Poached jobfish *à la mode* with parsley

•

Octopus curry in coconut cream, served with rice, mango and grated shark satini, pawpaw, *frizite* (prickly pear), lentils, eggplant and mixed vegetable pickle hashard. With *palmiste* millionaire's salad

•

Pamplemousse with burnt brown sugar
or
Breadfruit in coconut

•

Thé du Citronelle

Left: *The overgrown tangle around a long-deserted leper village on Curieuse.*

Praslin at a Glance

BEST TIMES TO VISIT

Try to avoid **December** to **February**, which are the rainy months. It can pour down, although rainfall on Praslin is slightly lower than on Mahé. Temperatures remain fairly constant at 30°C (86°F) and humidity 80%. At night the temperature can drop by as much as 6C° (11F°). There is always a breeze of around 6 to 7 knots increasing to 12 knots and more in **June** through **September**, the sailing season.

GETTING THERE

Although there are at least 15 **flights** daily from Mahé airport, these 15 minute flights cannot compare with the three hour trip on the inter-island **schooners** that take you back to the days of sail. Their timetable is:

Mon/Wed/Fri
La Belle Praslinoise Dep. 11:00
Cousin Dep. 13:00
Tues/Thurs
Cousin Dep. 12:00

There is not normally a service on Saturdays, Sundays and public holidays. No booking required. Try and arrive at the Inter-Islands ferry terminal in Victoria 30 minutes beforehand.
There are always taxis and buses waiting at Baie Ste Anne pier on Praslin.
You can also book a **helicopter** flight leaving from Victoria, tel: 375400.

GETTING AROUND

There are comfortable *Tata* **buses** that circle the island roughly every 45 minutes. Both sides of Praslin are relatively flat, and **bicycles** can be hired from both Côte d'Or (tel: 232071) and Grand'Anse (tel: 233033), or borrowed from your guest house. There are **taxis** and **car hire**. Try Standard, tel: 233555. The best way to see Praslin, however, is to **walk**.

WHERE TO STAY

The smallest accommodations are usually the most luxurious: **L'Archipel**. Southeast coast. Individual units in 20 acres of woodland by a secluded beach; tel: 232242, fax: 232072.
La Reserve. Northeast coast. Palm-thatched bungalows on the edge of the sea; tel: 232211, fax: 232166.
Chateau de Feuilles. South coast. Tucked away on a hill overlooking the sea; tel: 233316, fax: 233916.
Indian Ocean Lodge. Grand'Anse. More rustic but full of character. Thatched chalets, palms, fishing beach; tel: 233324, fax: 233911.
Maison des Palmes. Amitié, west coast. Thatched bungalows facing Cousin island; tel: 233411, fax: 233880.
Flying Dutchman. Grand'Anse, 13 chalets, good restaurant; tel: 233337, fax: 233993.
The large package holiday hotels have a good selection

of watersports. They include:
Praslin Beach Hotel. Côte d'Or beach, tel: 232222, fax: 232244.
Paradise Sun Hotel. Côte d'Or, tel: 232255, fax: 232019.
Côte d'Or Lodge, tel: 232200, fax 232130.
Coco de Mer. Southwest coast; tel: 233900, fax: 233919.

The excellent selection of small guest houses includes:
Beach Villa Guest house. Grand'Anse; tel: 233445.
Britannia. Grand'Anse, nice restaurant; tel: 233215, fax: 233944.
Cabane des Pêcheurs. Grand'Anse; nice beach views; tel: 233320.
Chalets Côte Mer. Baie Ste Anne; tel: 233867.
Le Grand Bleu. Self catering, two bedroom villa above Baie Ste Anne, tel: 233937.
Villa Flamboyant. Southwest coast, lovely trees on beach, specialises in painting holidays; tel: 233036, fax 233036.
Tiny **Chauve Souris** island just off Côte d'Or beach. Five rooms; tel: 232003, fax: 232133.
Beach Villa Guest house. Grand'Anse; tel: 233445.
Orange Tree Guest house. Baie Ste Anne; tel 233248.
My Dream. Little house facing Baie Ste Anne; tel: 232122.
The Islander. Four self catering villas. Anse Kerlan,

Praslin at a Glance

northwest coast; tel: 233224.
Le Duc de Praslin. Côte d'Or, east coast, three rooms; tel: 232252.

Where to Eat

All hotels and guest houses have restaurants. Also well worth trying:
Café des Arts on Côte d'Or beach. Excellent cuisine, an art gallery and an idyllic setting; tel: 232131.
Bonbon Plumes. Anse Lazio, north coast. Right on the exquisite powdery beach. Kreol food; tel: 232136.
Les Rochers. La Pointe, south coast. Lots of seafood; tel: 233034.
Flying Dutchman. Nice old sea salt pub; tel: 233337.
Black Parrot, in the large Coco de Mer hotel, Anse Bois de Rose, south coast; tel: 233900.
Archipel. At Anse Gouvernement, southeast coast, part of hotel; tel: 232242.
Laurier. Anse Volbert, east coast. Small, home cooking; tel: 232241.
Village du Pêcheur. On Côte d'Or beach, marvellous setting; tel: 232030.

Tours and Excursions

Mason's Travel has an office on Praslin (tel: 233211), as does TSS (tel: 233970), and National Travel Agency (tel: 233223).
Bird watching. Three-hour trips can be arranged to Cousin Island bird sanctuary with any of the above. Boat departures Tue, Thurs and Fri 09:00 from Grand'Anse.
Curieuse Marine Park. Day trip with lunch includes time on St Pierre and Curieuse Islands. Snorkelling equipment provided.
Scuba diving (and learning to dive). PADI courses, night dives, and wonderful coral and sea life in Curieuse Marine Park area. Contact Diving in Paradise, Anse Volbert, tel: 232148.
Watersports. Catamaran sailing, hobie cats, paddle skis, windsurfers etc. Praslin Beach Watersports. Anse Volbert near Côte d'Or, tel: 232148.
Vallée de Mai National Park. The tour operators undertake tours around the home of the coco de mer. Or take a taxi or bus, collect a map with your entrance fee and do it yourself.
Bus. An ideal way to see the island. Catch any normal bus, and take a picnic to the cove of your choice.
Bicycle. Praslin is an island of cyclists; hire one for the day and go right round the island. The only hill to try to avoid is over the Vallée de Mai between Grand'Anse and Baie Ste Anne.
Tours from Mahé. Tour operators' day trips to Praslin include hotel pickups, air or sea cruiser transfers, and transport to Vallée de Mai, Cousin, Curieuse Marine Park, or Aride island. Other tours combine Praslin and La Digue.

Useful Telephone Numbers

Tourist Information Offices: Mahé, tel: 225313 and airport, tel: 373136.
Air Seychelles: Praslin airport, tel: 233214.
Weather information: tel: 373377.
Health clinic: Grand'Anse, tel: 233414.
Hospital: Baie Ste Anne, tel: 233333.
Telephone operator: tel: 100.
Car hire: Standard (at Amitié, west coast near airport), tel: 233555; Austral (at Baie Ste Anne, near schooner jetty), tel: 232015; and others.
Taxis: Amitié airstrip, tel: 233429; Baie Ste Anne jetty, tel 233859.
Provisions: Luc's Super Store, Grand'Anse, tel: 233238. (Also for schooner enquiries).

PRASLIN	J	F	M	A	M	J	J	A	S	O	N	D
AVERAGE TEMP. °F	81	82	82	82	82	81	79	79	79	81	81	79
AVERAGE TEMP. °C	27	27.5	28	28	28	27	26	26	26.5	27	27	26.5
Hours of Sun Daily	5	6	7	8	8	8	8	7	7	8	7	6
SEA TEMP. °F	82	80	82	80	78	77	73	73	73	79	77	80
SEA TEMP. °C	28	27	28	27	26	25	23	23	23	26	25	27
RAINFALL in	12	7	6	5	5	4	2	4	5	6	7	12
RAINFALL mm	295	172	160	124	135	116	53	99	130	141	179	311
Days of Rainfall	9	5	6	6	6	3	3	4	4	5	5	10

5
La Digue and Islands Around Praslin

INDIAN OCEAN
Aride
Curieuse
Petite Soeur
Grande Soeur
Cousin
Félicité
Cousine
Praslin
Marianne
La Digue

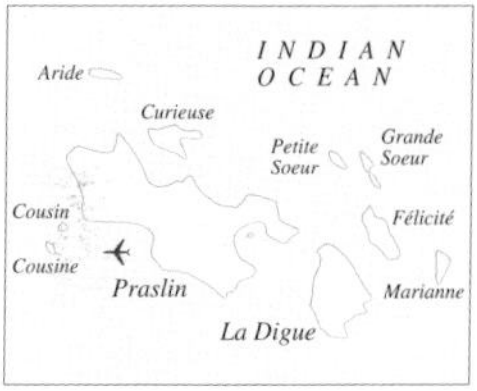

La Digue is chunky and different. Named after one of the French expeditionary sailing ships of 1768, the 2000 or so La Diguois would like to consider their island a separate republic. Here they travel in oxcarts on sand roads, there is no airport (although there is a helipad), they rely on white-sailed schooners to connect with the rest of the world, men go shirtless and shoeless, and even the Kreol language can be different.

La Digue, the fourth largest of the granitic islands, yet only 5km (3 miles) by 3km (2 miles) at its widest, lies a short schooner sail from Praslin's Baie Ste Anne. It is still the most traditional of the islands, although that and the addictive, rural atmosphere does make it increasingly attractive to visitors. There are about 10 hotels and guest houses on La Digue, and it is well within range for day trippers from Praslin, yet the tourists are still barely apparent. Once on the island there is nowhere more than an hour's walk away, although oxcarts, bicycles and horses are all used to get about. Only six cars and a minibus are allowed on the island.

La Digue is dominated by the 333m (1093ft) **Eagle's Nest** mountain and a broad, and at times marshy, agricultural plain on the northern side where most of the small population live. The island has spectacular black granite boulder formations, particularly along the beaches, curving and grooved as if by the hand of a giant sculptor. At times they can appear almost pink in colour. The beaches, inevitably, are wild, lonely, and beautiful, and in **La Digue Veuve Reserve**, the last known habitat

CLIMATE

La Digue can be very **wet** in December and January, when on the low-lying marshy plateau the mosquitoes (non-malarial) can be infuriating. It is **windy** from April to September in the southeasterly trade winds, the drier and more comfortable period. **Humidity** is 80% and **day-time temperatures** around 26°C (80°F). The best snorkelling and fishing times are from October until March.

Opposite: *Easy island days on one of La Digue's sandy highways.*

DON'T MISS

*** The schooner sail from Praslin. The first hint of traditional La Digue.
*** A ride in an oxcart. They're normally waiting at the schooner jetty.
** Walks to Grand'Anse, and around the island.
** A fishing trip on a small local boat.
** Cousin Island – bird and turtle reserve.
** Aride Island. Incredible birdlife and vegetation.
* La Veuve Paradise Flycatcher Reserve. Walk through the marshlands and past the lily ponds.
* Chateau St Cloud, and its tortoise pen. Stay for supper.

Below: *A schooner tied up to the jetty at La Passe.*
Opposite: *Decaying arrogance on the path to Grand'Anse.*

of the black paradise flycatcher, there is more evidence of Seychelles' incredible natural heritage. With a cat's cradle of tangled palms and takamakas leaning madcap over every gorgeous beach, colourful old tin colonial houses, white waves dashing against granite boulders, and haunting sunsets it is also the prime destination for fashion magazines, photographers and movie men. *Robinson Crusoe* was only one of several films shot on La Digue.

La Digue is one of 10 granitic islands grouped around Praslin. **Félicité**, to the northeast of La Digue, has a lodge located on its largest beach, but no other habitation. It was the island where the Sultan of Perak was exiled last century. The other islands near Praslin are largely uninhabited, although two, **Cousin** and **Aride**, are fascinating nature reserves, home to some of the rarest and largest of Seychelles' bird populations.

AROUND LA DIGUE
La Passe

La Passe, the main settlement on La Digue, takes its name from the one gap in the island's encircling reef which the schooners from Praslin use to get to the coral pier. In among the palms and takamakas arching over the road which follows the beach southwards from the pier are a number of colourful tin shops and buildings, including an art gallery, a new library, and Choppy's Bungalows. And a little further on a marshland of water lilies is the helipad, and a state farm with the largest vanilla plantation left in Seychelles. The atmosphere is so unhurried and simple it is difficult to believe much has changed since the first inhabitants, political exiles from the island of Réunion (near Mauritius), settled here and whose old graves can be seen in the cemetery at Cap Barbi.

A little way behind La Passe, visitors can find one of the real La Digue experiences in **Chateau St Cloud**, the old St Ange family house that sits overlooking La Réunion plain in the lee of the high forested Eagle's Nest mountain. It is now a delightful guest house run by the charismatic Kersley St Ange and his Malagasy wife Isabelle. It is an hour and a half's walk from the Chateau up the Belle Vue road to the summit of the island, **Nid D'Aigles** (which means Eagle's Nest, although there never have been any eagles in Seychelles), which offers a wonderful view of the necklace of granitic islands from Mahé round to Félicité.

Grand'Anse

A road crosses the island from the estate at L'Union to La Digue's version of Grand'Anse, and it is a popular walk. The flat lands are full of the island's traditional air, with the occasional single cow being led out to graze, an old plantation house at the end of a long avenue of palms, all rusting grey tin and decaying arrogance, and the studio of Constance, a wood craftsman

SEA MONSTER

The whale shark (*Rhinocodon typus*) is a totally harmless, cream-spotted blue monster that feeds on plankton.

● The whale shark has always terrified Seychelles fishermen, to whom it is known as *sagren* or grief. They believed the shark wraps itself around the anchor ropes of small pirogues and drags them under (such occurrences have been recorded).

● Whale sharks are usually only found off the coasts of Western Australia, Mexico and Seychelles, where the plankton density in the ocean is of festive proportions.

● At lengths of up to 15m (50ft), they are the largest fish in the world.

● Divers in Seychelles regularly swim alongside them.

whose carved panels are all over the island. On La Digue you are more likely to see the old plantation equipment and skills (such as rapid fire husking of coconuts on a stake in the ground) than anywhere else. Despite the increase in tourism, traditional industries such as patchouli, vanilla, copra, saffron, boat building and fishing are still very much a part of La Digue's way of life.

A huge old casuarina tree surrounded by grass and green veloutier bush stands sentinel on Grand'Anse, framed at either end by massive pinkish-black, grooved granite boulders. The beach faces the blustering southeast trades, and looks out towards Frégate Island, a blue silhouette in the ocean. Apart from the ghost crabs scurrying in the foaming surf there may only be a few pairs of wheeling fairy terns, a long-beaked turnstone, or a whimbrel, which migrates 10,000km (6000 miles) from Siberia. Though the sea, without the barrier of the coral reef, seems dramatic and inviting, take note of the multilingual warning sign about the currents.

The East Coast

Below: *The sun draws an unexpected grey sparkle from La Digue's corrugated granite rock.*

A track east through the palms goes over a small hill to another equally deserted and beautiful beach, **Petite Anse**, and then on along a series of thundering surf beaches around the back of the lush forested mountain.

La Digue's famous pink granite boulders are strewn around the edges of all these east coast beaches, giving colour both to the sand and the sparkling water lapping around their feet. One of the beaches, **Anse Caiman** (Crocodile Beach), is where the fearsome reptiles sat on the sands when the first French settlers arrived in 1798.

At **Anse Fourmis** the island's circular road begins again, weaving in and out of forest, coves, rocky outcrops and deserted beaches. It rounds the northern tip, where the views over the beaches, **Anse Gaulettes**, **Anse Patates, and Anse Sévère**, are a continuous delight, before leading back to La Passe.

Pointe Jacques

South from L'Union beach, a path leads to **Anse Source d'Argent**, a popular picnic spot. It carries on to **Anse Pierrot** and **Anse Bonnet Carré**, up to Pointe Jacques, the southerly tip of the island, where you will have to either scramble along the shore or over the headland. North from here there is a beach, **Grand l'Anse**, with a small island just off it, where the path becomes clearer again and joins the main road over the island between Grand'Anse itself and L'Union.

LA DIGUE VEUVE RESERVE

The plateau on La Digue between the mountain and the sea is dominated by Indian almond (*badamier*) trees, takamakas, and wetland. The marshes are the habitat of the

> **LILY OF THE ISLES**
>
> White, magenta and magnificent, the Seychelles lily, or in Kreol *lis dipei* (from the French: *lis du pays*) is probably the most beautiful of the many gorgeous and colourful Seychelles flowers. Its white petals with pink centre stripe grow in clusters of up to 20 trumpet-shaped flowers about 10cm (4in) in size. You will often see it in gardens or near the sea when walking about particularly on the seashore of the smaller islands and La Digue. Long evergreen leaves provide a bouquet for the flowers on their 61cm (2ft) high stalk.

Below: *The magnificent setting of wave-strafed Grand'Anse.*

BIRDS OF PARADISE

There are 30 species and sub-species of bird endemic to Seychelles, but as with island inhabitants the world over, they are all endangered.

● Seychelles blue pigeon. At a distance it looks like a fish-eagle; has a ko-ko-kok cry.

● Seychelles kestrel, or *katiti*. Tiny bird of prey that hides in the eaves of houses.

● Seychelles scops owl, or *syer*. Bare-legged resident of the high mountains. Rare and seldom seen.

● Seychelles black paradise flycatcher. Known as *vev*, and only found on La Digue. The white, orange and black female is totally different from the long-tailed blue black of the male.

Seychelles black paradise flycatcher, one of the most endangered birds in the world. There are perhaps only 50 pairs left, all on La Digue. Black-blue from the crown of its head to the tip of its long streamer tail, with a distinctive pale blue bill, the best place to see them is the tiny La Digue Veuve Reserve (*veuve*, or commonly just *vev*, which means 'widow' in Kreol, is the locals' name for the flycatchers).

The reserve is located by the road not far from Chateau St Cloud. Set up in a bid to save an area of natural habitat for the birds, the reserve has an information centre, a nature trail, and a permanent ranger. in the lily pools you might see the pale brown and orange **lily trotter,** or Chinese bittern, stalking across the swamp in search of some tiny bream or frogs. The ranger will also point out the best place to spot the rare **yellow-bellied and star-bellied terrapins**, known as *torti soupap* to the Seychellois, another species sadly endangered by the gradual draining of the marshes. These web-footed reptiles live in freshwater pools and marshes, and eat both plants and snails.

On the road leading down from the reserve to **L'Union** on the coast, there are more lily ponds, a giant tortoise pen, and mangroves where you might spot some wild orchids. L'Union, with its canopy of soaring, twisted palms, is the best beach on La Digue for

Right: *An oxcart, the principal form of transport on the island and the epitome of La Digue's stubbornly traditional way of life.*

snorkelling, and the thatched roof of the magnificent L'Union Plantation House is well worth a look. Horses can be hired at L'Union Estate, providing yet another popular and suitably relaxed way to see the island.

LA DIGUE ISLANDS

There are four small islands all within a radius of 7km (4 miles) of La Digue: Marianne, Félicité, Grande Soeur and Petite Soeur. The latter two, the **Sisters**, to the east of La Digue, are deserted. The larger, less than 2km (1 mile) long, has two attractive beaches either side of its hourglass middle. There is good fishing all around them, especially for barracuda and wahoo.

Above: *Chateau St Cloud, on Eagle's Nest mountain.*

Félicité Island

This island, half way between the two sisters and La Digue was, for five years in the late 19th century, the home of the exiled Sultan of Perak. These days isolation carries a healthy price tag, as it is probably the only place in the Seychelles outside the Amirantes where you can hire an island all to yourself. There are two lovely converted plantation houses, for one group booking only. The fishing is superb, particularly in and around the cluster of islets called Ile Cocos just off the northern shore of the island.

The island was a plantation run by the Cauvin family for many years and is now believed to be the favourite holiday spot for presidents and princes. The Félicité mountain rises steep above the little hook of beach and chalets, with a path to its 231m (760ft) summit, lush with gnarled old takamaka trees and coconuts, and some heart-stopping granite cliffs down to the sea.

CHATEAU ST CLOUD

This ancient two-storey grey and white stone chateau with creaking takamaka floors polished with manglier (an extract of mangrove), and multi-shuttered windows overlooking banks of flowers, breadfruit trees and a giant tortoise pen, would not be out of place in Provence or Blois, the regions of France the St Ange family left to come to Seychelles 200 years ago. Around the big dining table come evening, Isabelle produces a feast that only an island woman could conjure up, while Kersley cuts citronelle for the tea assuring everyone that it is essential for *l'amour*. Whereupon, kitted out in dark glasses, hat and guitar he serenades his guests in a send-up version of the local sentimental hit 'Goodbye Seychelles'.

SULTAN OF PERAK

The resident of Félicité for five years from 1877, the Sultan of Perak was one of the first of Seychelles distinguished list of exiles. He was banished from Perak, a territory on the Straits of Malacca in modern Malaysia, after organising the assassination of the British Resident there, James Birch.

Marianne Island

Named after one of the ships which came to Seychelles 200 years ago, Marianne is also uninhabited. It is thickly covered in coconuts but conservationists are hoping that the native forest will gradually return. There are some fine rock formations in the south, which can be seen from a boat, that are perhaps even better than La Digue's panoramic sculptures. The darting Seychelles sunbird *kolibri* is there in profusion.

Above: *An ebony pool in the heart of Félicité.*
Below: *A brown, or common, noddy.*

COUSIN

Cousin Island, lying 2km (1 mile) from Praslin's Anse Kerlan beach, is a little island covered in indigenous *mapou* and *bwa torti* forest, and a designated Special Reserve. It was purchased by the International Council for Bird Preservation in 1968 to protect its endangered and rare birds, particularly the **Seychelles brush warbler** (*le petit merle des iles* in French). Six people presently live on this island, which is much loved by nature conservationists and photographers.

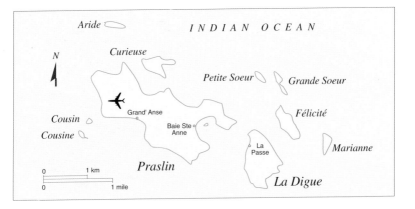

35,000 breeding **shearwaters**, large dark brown birds that bank low over the water between the waves, are protected on Cousin. Sometimes you can see 'rafts' of as many as a thousand shearwaters sitting on the water fishing for squid and flying fish, returning to their nests in the evening moaning and groaning. White **fairy terns** with little black beaks, **Audubons shearwater**, **frigate birds**, **tropic birds**, the Seychelles **turtle dove**, the little yellow-capped **fody**, or *tok tok* (from the sound of its cry) are all common on Cousin, together with Seychelles **blue pigeons**, **sunbirds** and 100,000 breeding **lesser noddys**.

Hawksbill turtles come to lay their eggs on Cousin's beaches from August to April. They are the subject of the world's longest running intensive monitoring programme of this species, with nearly 500 turtles tagged. The wardens have been known to risk their lives protecting these turtles from poachers, but in the last resort man may have to undertake the ranching of these beautiful and vulnerable sea creatures, as is done with many of Africa's wild animals, if they are to survive.

ARIDE

From banks of beautiful reefs and a tiara of white sand, Aride Island, 10km (6 miles) north of Praslin, rises in luxuriant guano-fed vegetation to a lovely plateau. It is a long green island of unbelievable beauty, which has been

---

NODDIES

There are two species of noddy tern in Seychelles: the lesser, a downy, dark-feathered sea bird, and the larger brown.
● Aride is the world's largest colony of lesser noddies, and Cousin the second largest.
● The brown, or common noddy, is found on a number of islands, including Aldabra. Its Kreol name is *makwa*, after its gutteral squawk.
● When things get too hot, the noddy will dash off to the ocean to dip her breast feathers in the water and return to cool down her large white egg.
● The fruit of the *pisonia grandis*, or *bwa mapou* tree, can cover a noddy with its sticky juice if it lands on the tree, preventing it from flying. It then starves.
● The word noddy is an old English term meaning foolish, or drowsy. The bird got the name because it was so easily captured by sailors.

Above: *A view from the road over to Baie Chevalier, on Praslin, looking out to Aride Island.*

WOBBLING WARBLER

Until recently, the Seychelles warbler wobbled on the knife-edge of extinction. The destruction of their habitat meant that in 1959 there were only 26 of these birds left. A campaign led by the International Council for Bird Preservation strove to save both the birds and their natural habitat on Cousin. It worked, and with a substantial population now installed on Aride, and numbers pushing the 500 mark, the warbler was recently taken off the Red Data list of endangered species.

---

preserved from the coconut planter's axe ever since it was first visited by man in 1756. The old Seychellois family Chenard owned it for 100 years and insisted it became a protected Seychelles sanctuary. In 1973 Aride Island Nature Reserve was purchased by Christopher Cadbury (of the chocolate family) for the Royal Society for Nature Conservation, and in 1975 it became a Special Reserve.

Aride, even more so than Cousin, is Seychelles' great bird paradise. Only Aldabra boasts more varieties of breeding sea bird, and between May and October over a million birds lay their eggs on the island. It is home to more **lesser noddys** than anywhere else in the world, an unusual hilltop **sooty tern** colony, and a total of 10 species of breeding sea birds. Among the granitic islands, only Aride plays host to breeding **red-tailed tropic birds**. There are also big populations of **white-tailed tropic bird**, **fairy terns**, **shearwater** and the huge, evil-looking **frigate birds**.

The English artist and botanist Marianne North, who came exploring the Seychelles in the 1880s, visited Aride to paint **Dr Wright's gardenia**. Known as *bwa sitron* in

Kreol this shrub has a heavenly scent, trumpet-shaped white flowers flecked with magenta, and a hard round green fruit. Some 1300 still grow on Aride, but nowhere else on earth. Among a long list of other ecological claims, Aride has more **lizards** per square metre than anywhere else in the world, and recently discovered, some cucumber-like **peponium**, the water gourd of the Greeks. As it is not too far from Cousin, it is also a haven for breeding **hawksbill turtles**. The crystal blue waters around the island are equally prolific with some 150 species of **coral fish**.

Aride is one of the most memorable islands in Seychelles. Visits to the island are controlled both by the warden and the weather, which can make landing difficult. Ashore, there are a number of trails which lead to viewing points, the beach at La Cour, and through some of the island's untouched forest.

Such protected habitat could be of great value to some of Seychelles' more endangered wildlife and plant species. Already some of Cousin's fast disappearing warblers have been very successfully translocated, and with the positive attitude of much of Seychelles conservation, further successes can be anticipated.

Travel Agents in Seychelles organise regular trips to Aride, but there is no accommodation for visitors.

COCONUT SUPREME

There are two million coconut trees in Seychelles. These languid palms, leaning crazily over beach and sea, have all sorts of uses:
- The nut is eaten, squeezed into a cream, or even grilled as a cocktail snack.
- Perfume, margarine, soap and sunscreens contain coconut oil.
- The brittle shell, ground and turned into a charcoal paste, lubricates aircraft bearings. It is also fuel for fire.
- Mattresses, anchor ropes, and car seats all benefit from coconut husk coir. Used as a plaited trace by Seychelles fishermen in pre-nylon days.
- Mahé matrons do a sort of sega dance as they polish floors with a sliced half-husk.
- Seychelles shopping bags, heart-shaped fans and roof thatch all make use of the strong fronds.
- Tasty dainties include heart of palm salad, sweet germinating nut, and young cocotane milk.
- The sap of the tree, toddy or *calou*, tastes initially like ginger beer. Leave it 12 hours and it will blow your head off.
- Coconut palm fronds serve as makeshift sails, beach picnic cloths, and firewood for heating moutia drums.

Left: *A hawksbill turtle. On Cousin Island they are successfully monitored and protected.*

La Digue and Praslin Islands at a Glance

BEST TIMES TO VISIT

During the **December** to **February** rainy season, the low-lying plateau of La Digue where most of the hotels are sited can be very wet, with some parts flooding. The best times to visit are **April** to **September** when it is less humid and the southeast trades are blowing. Because of its dense forests it always seems more tropical on La Digue. The temperatures, in the main, are the same as the other granitic islands, an average of 27°C (81°F) and 80% humidity.

GETTING THERE

There is no airport on La Digue, but there is a **helipad** in a clearing among the palms with shuttle services three times a week. The normal route is to fly by plane to Praslin and take the regular **schooner ferry** from Baie Ste Anne, a half-hour trip that sails three times a day, though not on Saturdays and only two on Sundays. These sometimes run more frequently, depending on demand. There is one schooner ferry direct from Mahé at 13:00 on Mondays, Wednesdays and Fridays and 12:00 on Tuesdays and Thursdays. No weekend service, but it's always worth checking in Victoria with Inter-island Ferry Service, tel: 233229 or 233859.

Trips to the **smaller islands**, Aride, Curieuse, Cousin etc, can be arranged through the main Seychelles tour operators: **Mason's Travel**, tel: 322642 (Victoria), 233211 (Praslin), 234227 (La Digue); **NTA**, tel: 224900 (Victoria), 233223 (Praslin), 234340 (La Digue); **TSS**, tel: 322414 (Victoria), 233438 (Praslin), 234110 (La Digue). Luxury yachts, catamarans, and motor cruisers can be hired from **Marine Charter** in Victoria, tel 322126.

GETTING AROUND

There are only half a dozen cars on La Digue and a minibus. The normal modes of transport on the island are oxcart and bicycles. The **oxcarts**, pulled by Brahman bulls, will transport you and your luggage when you arrive at the schooner pier. **Bicycles** can be hired from several operators near the pier at La Passe, including Rent-A-Bicycle, tel: 234250. Also check with guest houses. The roads are all sand and they are great for **walking**.
There are only walking tracks on the **smaller islands**, although the local manager or one of his labourers will probably lend you a bicycle.

WHERE TO STAY

There are 10 establishments on La Digue. They include:
Chateau St Cloud. Enchanting old two-storey plantation residence. Superb value. Run like a sociable country inn at the time of the French Revolution; with its own resident giant tortoises; tel: 234346, fax: 234346.
La Digue Island Lodge. Anse Réunion beach. Luxury palm thatched A-frames, with pool. Family run, upmarket, trips arranged to Félicité island; tel: 234232, fax: 234100.
Patatran Village. Luxury guest house recently built on a rise overlooking Anse Patates beach and Félicité Island. Seven double chalets; tel: 234333, fax: 225273.
Choppy's Bungalows. At Anse Réunion. Four rooms, long established, Kreol cuisine, popular pub; tel: 234224, fax: 234088.
Bernique Guest house (with self-catering annex). La Réunion. 10 minutes walk inland, good restaurant; tel: 234229, fax: 234288.

Félicité Island:
Félicité is a short sea voyage from Praslin or La Digue. Félicité Island Lodge has two luxurious colonial style bungalows under thatch, air-conditioning and a tennis court. Group bookings only. tel: 234233, fax: 234100.

There are a variety of small guest houses, mainly inland in the La Passe and Anse Réunion areas:
Jonc d'Or Guest house; tel: 234250.
Paradise Fly Catcher Villas, self catering; tel:234015.
Villa Mon Rêve, tel: 234218.
Sunshine, only 3 rooms; tel: 234033.

La Digue and Praslin Islands at a Glance

Citronnelle, self catering, 2 rooms; tel: 234240.
Note: There are no accommodation facilities on Aride, Cousin, Cousine, Curieuse or any islands surrounding Praslin and La Digue other than Félicité. Ornithologists wishing to stay overnight on any of these bird sanctuaries should write for advice to: Adrian Skerrett, Box 336, Mahé; fax: 322978; or to the Director General, Ministry of the Environment, Box 445, Mahé; fax: 224500.

WHERE TO EAT

Patatran. Anse Sévère. 15 minutes along coastal road by bicycle. Good value Kreol food; tel: 234180.
La Digue Island Lodge. Anse Réunion. Elegant palm thatched dining room, poolside bar; tel: 234232.
Bernique. Spicy Kreol food. Anse Réunion; tel: 234229.

All the guest houses will take diners if you give them a little notice. It is usually in these small family-run establishments that you will get not only the best value, but also the more unusual Kreol dishes. Again, nearly all restaurants and guest houses are sited on the easily-walked circular route from La Passe inland to Chateau St Cloud, then back to the shore again at Anse Réunion. Try **Tournesol,** tel: 234155; **Villa Mon Rêve,** tel: 234218; or **Sunshine,** tel: 234033.

TOURS AND EXCURSIONS

The three big tour operators will assist you with any excursion, hotel booking, bicycle hire, or holiday activity. All have offices at La Passe on La Digue. **Mason's Travel,** tel: 234227; **TSS,** tel: 234110; and **National Travel Agency,** tel: 234340.
Day trips from Mahé by schooner or helicopter include a visit to L'Union thatched Plantation House. Can also be combined with visits to or from Praslin.
Diving. Many good locations. La Digue Island Lodge has a dive centre. Also try La Passe Diving Centre near the pier.
Sailing. Hobie cats and windsurfers available at La Digue Island Lodge.
Félicité Island excursion. La Digue Island Lodge will arrange a day trip to this lovely island.
Fishing. Barracuda, wahoo, tuna, and bonito are plentiful particularly between Félicité and Les Soeurs, while fishing in a small boat off the reefs is exhilarating. All hotels and guest houses have a favourite fisherman and all can arrange fishing trips.

Snorkelling. Best to bring your own equipment, but it can usually be borrowed or hired from the larger hotels.
Horse riding. Contact L'Union Estate, tel 234240.
Ox-cart trips. Inexpensive and available anywhere along the main roads. Leisurely way to see the countryside and meet the villagers.
The **La Digue Festival** takes place on 15 August each year, Assumption Day. It is a grand day with bunting, processions, music, feasting and festivities. It is very popular, attracting folk from Mahé and Praslin, as well as practically all the residents of La Digue.

USEFUL TELEPHONE NUMBERS

Tourist Information Office, Mahé, tel: 225313 and 373136 (Mahé Airport).
Air Seychelles (Inter-island), tel: 373101.
Logan Hospital, La Digue, tel: 234255.
Post Office (Near pier at La Passe), tel: 234036.
Telephone enquiries: tel: 100.
Barclays Bank, tel: 234148.
Police, La Passe, tel: 234251.
Emergency, tel: 999.

LA DIGUE	J	F	M	A	M	J	J	A	S	O	N	D
AVERAGE TEMP. °F	81	82	82	82	82	81	79	79	79	81	81	79
AVERAGE TEMP. °C	27	27.5	28	28	28	27	26	26	26.5	27	27	26.5
Hours of Sun Daily	5	6	7	8	8	8	8	7	7	8	7	6
SEA TEMP. °F	82	80	82	80	78	77	73	73	73	79	77	80
SEA TEMP. °C	28	27	28	27	26	25	23	23	23	26	25	27
RAINFALL in	12	6	7	6	5	3	3	6	5	8	6	12
RAINFALL mm	315	149	178	146	129	84	87	124	124	203	154	313
Days of Rainfall	9	5	6	6	5	3	3	3	3	4	5	9

6
A Pattern of Islands

From granite mountains to coral specks, huge atolls to little more than a ring of sand and a solitary palm, there are 115 islands in Seychelles stretching like a string of pearls across 1000km (620 miles) of the Indian Ocean. Away from the main island group around Mahé and Praslin, the Seychelles archipelago quickly becomes remote and unknown, yet these Outer Islands are as rich as their more populous siblings, and just as valuable a part of the vivid tapestry of the archipelago.

The vast majority are uninhabited, and visitors common on just a few. To get to any of them is both difficult and adventurous, but for that the rewards seem all the greater. The names of the **Amirantes, Alphonse, Farquhar,** and possibly the most fascinating of all, **Aldabra,** are ones to conjure up images of wildness and wonder, endless sky, sea and floating islands. They are places where nature is still strongly in command, where unique plants and unusual animals cling to a thin thread of existence, not always threatened by man, but often simply by the wheels of nature itself.

BIRD ISLAND
Bird, the most northerly of the Seychelles islands, is a nugget of coral, palms, turquoise tropical sea, and a million breeding seabirds. Everyone has their favourite island in Seychelles, and for many who have managed to get there only once, this is Bird.

As you get off the Otter aircraft after a half-hour flight from Mahé, Georges and Margaret Norah are there to

CLIMATE

The **rainfall** is higher in the granitic islands of Silhouette, Frégate and around Mahé than in the hotter and drier coral islands like Bird, the Amirantes chain and the great atolls of the south: Aldabra, Cosmoledo and Farquhar. The latter can experience **cyclones** in the northwesterly monsoon from December to February. Very few of the coral islands have the forests of the granitic group but all have shady palms and casuarinas, and as low islands in a wide sea they have refreshing **breezes** whatever the season.

Opposite: *Poivre atoll.*

DON'T MISS

*** The experience of staying at one of the remote and luxurious island lodges. The islands become all yours.
*** A few days with the birds on Bird Island.
*** A sail to the Amirantes. Each evening a new island.
** The thrill of fishing for sailfish and marlin.
** A walk on coral mushrooms on Aldabra.
** Scuba diving anywhere. A thousand corals, a thousand fish in magic technicolour and crystal clear water.
** The walk over Silhouette's Dauban mountain. Lush mist forests and some magical untouched flora.
* The island of Frégate: maybe your best chance for pirate treasure in Seychelles.

greet you. Georges explains that the essence of Bird is in what it doesn't have. No airconditioning, no TV, no telephones in rooms and no need to lock anything away. The wood and coconut thatch bungalows are new; the old ones were getting washed away by a cantankerous sea and now provide windswept breeding perches for fairy terns. The lodge has a library, a shop, and even a farm and piggery that produce all the lodge's vegetables and fruit. Even the bar was made out of East Borneo camphor wood washed ashore one stormy night.

Bird Island was originally called Ile aux Vaches, after the dugongs, or seacows, that early French explorers found here. Although there are no dugongs left, there certainly are birds. The island is an endless whirl of them: **fairy terns**, with blue-black beaks and eyes gleaming out of a cloak of white, perch in cuddling couples in the eaves of your bungalow, grey-brown **noddy terns** dominate the seashore, and between May and October each year half a million chattering, crying, and wheeling black-and-white **sooty terns** arrive to breed and sit on their speckled eggs.

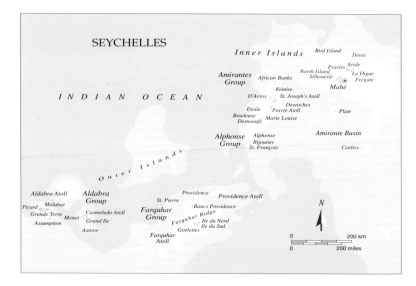

SEYCHELLES

Inner Islands   Bird Island   Denis

Amirantes Group   African Banks   Praslin   Aride
North Island   Silhouette   La Digue
Frégate
Mahé

I N D I A N   O C E A N   · Rémire
D'Arros   ·· St. Joseph's Atoll
·· Desroches
Etoile   ·Poivre Atoll   · Plate
Boudeuse   · Marie Louise
Desnoeufs

Alphonse Group   Alphonse
Bijoutier   *Amirante Basin*
St. François   Coétivy ·

O u t e r   I s l a n d s

Aldabra Atoll   *Aldabra Group*   Providence   Providence Atoll
Picard   Malabar   Cosmoledo Atoll   St. Pierre   :Bancs Providence
Grande Terre   Menai   Grand Ile   *Farquhar Group*   Farquhar Ridge
Assumption   Astove   Goëlettes   Ile du Nord
Ile du Sud
Farquhar Atoll

N

0   200 km
0   200 miles

Each guest receives a check list which includes the common **crab plover, sanderling, swallow, great frigate,** and **wedge-tailed shearwater**. In addition, the dedicated ornithologists can hope to see the **black cuckoo, broad-billed sandpiper** and **corncrake**. Wherever you walk on the island there is the cry of seabirds. They nest up trees, on the grass and fringing the lip of the high-rise beach, a myriad dots of black against the snow-white sand. Even the Lodge itself is shaped like a giant frigate bird.

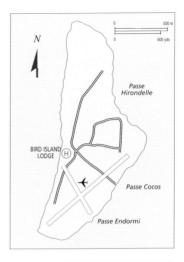

Around Bird Island

At the northern sandbank on the island the open beach reveals nothing but sooty terns. They dive and hover a metre above you, their masked faces curious and inquisitive. Their nest is a simple open 'scrape' of sand; if you are gentle they will allow you to get quite close. Before the island was declared a wildlife sanctuary in 1986, this placid attitude was exploited by egg collectors. There are five major sooty tern colonies in Seychelles: on Bird, Aride, Desnoeufs, Cosmoledo and Farquhar.

Bird only covers 69ha (170 acres), and at most it takes two hours to walk around its encircling white on white

MERMAIDS

The dugongs, or seacows, that gave Bird Island its original name, are sea mammals not dissimilar to manatees, their American cousin. Their wailing, mournful cries were thought by early mariners to be those of maidens, and so the legend of the singing mermaid (sometimes known as a siren) was born. Dugongs are herbivores, and suckle their young in human fashion above the water, a fact which may well have further established the romantic tales. Although there are no dugongs left in Seychelles, there are still some along the East Coast of Africa, and they may yet return to the islands.

Left: *The beach on the western side of Bird Island, in front of the bungalows.*

beach with grey smooth driftwood sticking up out of the sand. Sky blue waters surround the island which is bounded by jagged reef at **Passe Coco** and **Passe Hirondelle** on the eastern side. The island is a wildlife sanctuary and a 20-year bird research project is underway at the moment.

Bird is on the fathomless edge of the Seychelles bank, and consequently the deep-sea fishing off it is particularly good. At night the absence of lights and land make for a magnificent sweep of stars. And one friend you'll definitely make is **Esmeralda,** the island's pet tortoise. Weighing in at 298kg (657lb), Esmeralda (she is actually a he) is recorded in the Guinness Book of Records as the largest tortoise in the world. The Aldabran giant land tortoise has been known to live up to 150 years, though Bird Islanders staunchly maintain that Esmeralda is over 200. A forceful personality, he wanders around from chalet to chalet content to take titbits from guests.

DEEP-SEA FISHING

Game, or fighting fish, such as black marlin, blue marlin, tuna, wahoo, bonita and barracuda, are all found in Seychelles waters, along with the prince of them all, the sailfish, which features on Seychelles' coat of arms. The best months for sailfish are March to June, October and November. A number of boats are available to charter for fishing, with skippers who know the waters well. Speak to your hotel, or Marine Charter, who will arrange charters on local boats.

ILE DENIS

Governor Sweet-Escott, doing his rounds of the islands by boat in 1903, came to Denis, the guano-rich, and hence verdant, coral island 16km (10 miles) east of Bird. There he found that the lighthouse was 'in capital order and the

Above: *Esmeralda.*
Right: *A pair of fairy terns.*

quarters of the lightkeeper much improved'. The lighthouse, refurbished in 1910, is still there but the accommodations have changed out of all recognition. The 24 thatched chalets of the **Denis Island Lodge** on this mile-long coral island are luxurious, and the cuisine of the present owner, French industrialist Pierre Burkhardt, is as good as any in Seychelles.

Denis was named after sea captain Denis de Trobriand, who anchored off its ring of blue water and snowy beach in his vessel *L'Etoile* on 11 August 1773, en route to India. In more recent years the Rassool family, of Iranian descent, ran the coconut plantation that grows thickly right across the island. Sited on the edge of the Seychelles Bank, which disappears into a 2000m (6500ft) abyss, the fishing for marlin and sailfish is always good, and the island has become very popular with deep-sea fishermen. Denis has several unusual touches: its time is one hour ahead of the rest of Seychelles, there are two abandoned prisons, it has a chapel, and some unusual and interesting coral formations known as the Caves.

COWRIES

Of the 165 known species of cowrie, a mollusc, 50 can be found in Seychelles.
• Cowries are the homes of living creatures that feed on algae. The fleshy mantle of the animal creates the hard, glossy shell.
• The name originates from the Hindu word *kauri*; the shells have often been used as a form of currency.
• Two of the most common cowries in Seychelles are the tiger, and the Arabian cowrie.

Above: *The chalets of Denis Island Lodge.*
Left: *The airstrip and northern end of Denis.*

GETTING TO SILHOUETTE

Before helicopters and the building of the long jetty which now provides access to the island, getting to Silhouette was quite a hazardous affair. As its name suggests, La Passe was the way in, but having to judge the swell and the jagged coral teeth was nerve-wracking and fraught with danger. Today, boats anchor off and a rubber dinghy makes the short transfer to the newly-built jetty. There are only three boats weekly, and day trips are discouraged.

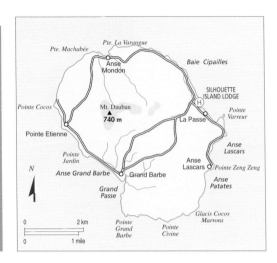

SILHOUETTE

Silhouette stands as a ghostly, mist-capped pyramid in a silvery sea, a shrouded dark shape against the sunset. It is the island you see from Beau Vallon Bay on Mahé, Seychelles' high-forested answer to Bali Hai in the South Pacific. Only 19km (12 miles) from Mahé, it is the third largest island in the archipelago, and the only one with mist forests as high as on Mahé. The highest point is the 740m (2428ft) Mount Dauban. Silhouette gives its name to Air Seychelles's inflight magazine, but the name of the island in fact came from a French finance comptroller, Etienne de Silhouette, rather than its moody, darkened profile.

Silhouette was owned for many years by the Dauban family, and has been relatively untouched by both the planter's axe and the developer's foundation stone. It has no airstrip and no regular ferry service other than a helicopter to the luxury lodge and power-boats to the jetty. You will, however, get espresso coffee and pasta, as the island's one lodge is Italian run.

Opposite: *The green-fringed lagoon on Silhouette.*
Left: *Silhouette in its most common guise: mist-capped and dominating the view from Beau Vallon on Mahé.*

DAUBAN, QUIXOTE OF SILHOUETTE

Buried in an impressive Grecian-columned mausoleum on Silhouette are generations of Daubans who have owned and run the island since 1864. Auguste Dauban, who fought at Waterloo, was the first to settle here. For much of this century his bachelor descendant Henri Dauban, a tall, gaunt planter, intellectual, and environmentalist ran Silhouette. A graduate of the London School of Economics, he joined the British Olympic javelin team in 1924, despite the fact that he was a Frenchman. He was an expert pirogue builder and excellent chef. The old family plantation house, built of indigenous hardwoods, still stands at La Passe on Silhouette.

The island was known to Arab seamen (or *lascars* as they are called in Seychelles), a thousand years ago. Graves and ruins at Anse Lascars are believed to be of Arab origin but it will probably take sophisticated archaeological examination to confirm this. Ships of the English East India Company sighted Silhouette in 1609, while 200 years later Le Corsair Hodoul spent some time here. It is claimed (as it is for practically every island in Seychelles) that he buried treasure on one of its beautiful beaches.

Around Silhouette

Silhouette is roughly round in shape, 5km (3 miles) long by 4km (2.5 miles) wide, and is completely surrounded by reef. No money is used in the island's one and only shop, as the island's 200 copra workers simply sign for what they want. There are no bicycles, roads or oxcarts, but there is a small clinic, school, and, at Séme, a lovely church.

Mont Dauban mountain is a tropical mist forest crammed with botanical treasure, including the rare pitcher plant with its secret juices which dissolve insects. Tiny orchids and rare hardwoods such as *bwa rouz* and *bwa-d-nat* grow there, while the rare incense tree *bwa sandal* is only found on Silhouette. Other Silhouette specials include the *trilepisium madagascariense*, or false fig tree, discovered in 1883 on Mont Dauban, probably by the indefatigable Marianne North. The state farm on Silhouette is exceptionally

productive, sending goats, chickens and vegetables to
Mahé. Nearby is a lovely lagoon surrounded by palms
and mangroves. High in the lush rocky mountains, on
the trail from **La Passe** to **Grand Barbe**, you can see fruit-
bats hanging from the trees or gliding like a prehistoric
pterodactyl, the sun catching the leathery sheen of their
wings. There are a number of trails on the island, around
the rocky coast or up through the thick, mostly
untouched high forests.

North Island

The first westerners ever to set foot on Seychelles did so
on North Island in 1609 when a group of Englishmen
from the *Ascension* landed. Led by Commander
Alexander Sharpeigh of the East India Company, the
longboats brought back
the giant tortoises to eat
that John Jourdain, whose
diary records the islands
for the first time, claimed
looked 'soe uglie before
they were boyled'.

Above: *A sooty tern.*
Below: *Waves pounding
in on tiny North Island.*

Source of much fruit
and guano in plantation
days, North Island is now
a favourite of deep-sea
fishermen. Located just
beyond Silhouette, the

6km (4 mile) long island is also granitic, though not nearly as verdant as its larger neighbour. There are no facilities on the island, but it does have lovely beaches at **Grand'Anse** and **Anse Cimitière**, or Cemetery. In the days before helicopters, when inter-island transport was by 12-man pirogue, an ill child would often die before the men could row the 25km (15 miles) of open ocean to the doctor on Mahé. To this day you will see little crosses on the outer islands. **Grand Paloss** mountain dominates this unprotected, wave-lashed pinnacle of an island locked on the edge of the seas.

FREGATE

This small island is the most remote of the granitic group, 56km (34 miles) east of Mahé. It used to have the only game on Seychelles, asiatic deer imported from Mauritius, and now has giant tortoises living in the wild. Its main exports have always been rum, copra, cashew nuts, vegetables and the myth of pirate treasure.

Unlike Silhouette or North it has an airstrip, and there is a lodge for visitors based at the old **Etablissement Plantation House**, surrounded by trees. You actually enter the Plantation House through the aerial roots of an Indian banyan tree.

As to buried treasure, Frégate comes tantalisingly close to the real thing. A sunken well lined with lead, ruins, cannonballs and gold have all apparently been found, and coral tombs have been reported. In 1812 a cross-belt and shoulder strap were unearthed, while in 1838 one visitor recorded that 'Spanish piastres and other coins called cruzados have been found on the shore ... with calm weather one can distinguish, half a mile from land, the debris of a large ship which lies at the bottom of the sea'. Careful research may yet reveal that all these finds are linked to

---

CORAL REEF FISH

There are 1000 species of reef fish in Seychelles:
● Parrot fish: bright blending colours. Named after their parrot beaks.
● Razor fish: these thin, pencil-like creatures swim in a vertical handstand position.
● Blue angelfish: a flat, square fish with iridescent blue edging to its wings.
● Moorish idol: gorgeous zebra markings and white top streamer.
● Batfish, or *pouldo* in Kreol. As large as a tennis racquet, and will swim alongside you.

Below: *The tropical charm of Frégate.*

HERCULES

- The Latin name of Frégate's huge tenebrionid beetle is *pulposipes herculeanus.*
- Its Kreol name is *bib arme*, which means armed spider, but despite its knobbly, spidery legs, it is a beetle.
- European entomologists seeing specimens for the first time were convinced that it was a hoax, stuck together from bits of other insects.
- It is found only on Frégate.

the Arab seamen who crossed the Indian Ocean in their graceful dhows a thousand years ago, a treasure trove for archaeologists at least, if not bounty hunters.

In the hinterland forest are lovely dragon's blood trees, their splayed trunks the favourite crawling territory of Frégate's unique **giant tenebrionid beetle**, which looks like a steel plated version of the African dung beetle.

Flowers are a feature of Frégate, and birders come to Frégate, with its lonely beaches and promontories of grooved rocks, to see the all but extinct **Seychelles magpie robin**. There are only 22 of these birds left in the world, all on Frégate. They are tame ground feeders with a blue sheen and white feather patches that can be seen as they fly. In Frégate it is known as *'ti santerz,* or the little singer. The rare Seychelles fody (found only on Frégate, Cousin and Cousine), as well as the Seychelles blue pigeon, a colourful bird with a fish eagle-like white stole, can be spotted on the island.

AMIRANTES

'And after some months here we fight, perhaps a bit feebly, against a desire to forget about the world at large rather than against a desire to be in the midst of things again'. So wrote New Yorker Wendy Veevers-Carter in 1966 about life on **Rémire Island** in the fabulous Amirantes, a chain of tiny coral atolls covered with palms

Below: *Coral reef, island and ocean. An aerial view of Desroches, one of the Amirantes atolls.*

Amirantes Group   `Mahé`

Alphonse
Group

Aldabra
Group   I N D I A N
                         O C E A N

Farquhar Group

Left: *Sooty terns, covering the rough coral surface and filling the air of Desnoeufs like clouds of insects.*

in the middle of the Indian Ocean, another world apart. Tragedy struck Veevers-Carter when her husband died on a trip to East Africa; being so remote she only learnt of his death weeks later. Their Spanish-style bungalow, now in ruins, stands facing the pass in the reef on this lovely round island.

Rémire is only one in a chain of 25 islands stretching south across 100km (62 miles) of ocean halfway between Mahé and Aldabra. From **Boudeuse** ('the sulky one'), to **Marie Louise**, **St Joseph** with its cluster of islets thick with coconut palms, and **D'Arros**, the horizon seems to promise a new island everytime you raise anchor. To visit these emerald jewels in a magic sea is an experience that will haunt you for ever.

The Amirantes were known to Arab seamen and were named in 1502 in honour of Vasco da Gama. It takes 24 hours to sail the 250km (155 miles) from Mahé to Rémire, the faint tuft tops of palms being the first warning of land on the horizon. The warning wasn't always heeded, as there have been many wrecks in the Amirantes. One of the earliest recorded was that of H.M.S. *Fire* in 1801, after which one Lieutenant Campbell, the commander, successfully sailed to Mahé in a canoe to get help.

Although airstrips have been built on several of the islands, only four are inhabited, and **Desroches** alone

VASCO DA GAMA

The name of Portuguese sailor Vasco da Gama is one of the most important in the annals of early European exploration of the globe. Less than a decade after Columbus had reached the West Indies, Da Gama set out to find a seaborne route to the East Indies in a bid to break the Muslim stronghold on the spice trade. His first voyage in 1497/8 took him round the Cape of Good Hope and up the East African coast, before crossing to reach the coast of India at Calicut. He was made an admiral just before his second voyage, which took him to Goa, which was to become the centre of Portuguese power in the East.

Above: *The bared and rusting bones of a shipwreck on Desnoeufs.*

has been developed. A luxury lodge and a satellite ground station enable this island to lay claim to being 'the doorway to the Amirantes'. A copra plantation is still working on the island, along with timber stands, and wood and charcoal are sent to Mahé. There is a small village of around 50 people, while the lodge has 20 chalets and offers some exciting watersports, especially diving.

Many islands are not inhabited at all, although at one stage or another most have been exploited for coconuts, green turtle, shark, timber, green snail (mother of pearl shells), and above all, guano. The removal of this dung deposited by tens of millions of birds over thousands of years (particularly during the last ice age when millions of seabirds fled south) has badly affected some islands, leaving them covered with a coral pavement which one has to break through to reach the water table.

The uninhabited, 35ha (86 acres) **Desnoeufs**, with a sooty tern colony three times that of Bird Island, was formerly the source of vast quantities of eggs, though now the island is enjoying a degree of protection as a breeding reserve.

Poivre

One of the loveliest of the islands is Poivre, named after Pierre Poivre, the man who encouraged the planting of spices in Seychelles. He is to be distinguished from Pierre Poiret, the man who claimed to be the true heir of Marie Antoinette and Louis XVI. Poiret farmed on the island between 1804 and 1822. A long lagoon, rich in bird song and lush vegetation, cuts into the atoll. To pole the length of this lagoon in the early morning with fairy terns wheeling above the trees, waders strutting, an occasional turtle rising and perhaps even a giant guitarfish wriggling away beneath your boat, can be quite inspiring.

PIERRE POIVRE

His name literally translates as Peter Pepper, but perhaps he is more widely remembered as Peter Piper, the man who picked a peck of pickled pepper. A peck was a barrel which had a volume of about 9 litres (2 gallons). He was the first intendant on the Ile de France, the name of Mauritius during French rule, and believed that on both Mauritius and Seychelles he could grow spices to compete with the lucrative trade that was being conducted between the East Indies and Europe.

At low tide you can walk
across the sand from La
Pointe to Poivre Island
itself, where handsome
bwa blanc trees shade the
manager's old, sparse
La kaz (cage) house.
Accommodation on Poivre
is very basic.

Alphonse Group
The smaller Alphonse
group of atolls, three in all,
lies 90km (56 miles) fur-

Above: *Casuarina trees by a crusty coral beach on St François atoll.*

ther south and 400km (250 miles) from Mahé. **Alphonse**
itself is a shovel-shaped island of extraordinary beauty
surrounded by perfect coral reef gardens. Small paths
circle the island; at either tip, Dot and Tamatave, there
are shipwrecks. **Bijoutier**, which means bejewelled, and
St François complete this little deserted cluster available
only to those with sail, compass, and a fair bit of time.

FAR OUT ISLES
Ile Plate (Flat Island) and Coétivy are in the opposite
direction to the Amirantes from Mahé, and roughly as far
away. **Plate** is renowned for its fishing and broad sandy
beaches at either end of its 1.5km (1 mile) length. It seems

Below: *St Joseph's atoll. An aerial photograph reveals the extent of the submerged coral reef around the island.*

NEW YEAR ON COÉTIVY

Travel writer F.D. Ommaney came to Coétivy at the end of 1947. As they departed on their boat, bonfires had been lit on the shore, he wrote, and the new year fiesta had begun, while in the little deckhouse cabin '... we drank to 1948 in an old schooner loaded with copra and crawling with inquisitive little beetles. The crew were heaving on the capstan by the glimmer of a lamp on the forestays...under the first stars of the new year the *Diolinda* spread her dusky wings and slipped into the night'.

Above: *Rough coral pinnacles with sand dunes rising behind, on the shoreline of Aldabra.*
Below: *A hermit crab, in its borrowed home.*

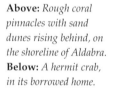

to emerge as if from nowhere out of a vast expanse of ocean, and many a mariner has come to grief on its reef.

Coétivy covers an area of 931ha (3.5 sq miles), a long thin island 10km (6 miles) long and one of the most productive islands both from sea and land in Seychelles. It is from Coétivy that the restaurants of Mahé get their tiger prawns, the delicious *krevet*, a commercially grown prawn which is also exported. Pork, beef, copra, fish, fruit, lamb and an abundance of vegetables are produced on the agriculturally rich soil of Coétivy, something that visitors have noted for years. Bishop Vincent Ryan in 1859 recorded that there were spacious pigsties on the island with 'immense animals in them' while the coconut mill employed 45 donkeys.

The island was first visited by a French sea captain named Coétivy in 1771. The old building ashore has thick walls and doors carved out of heavy takamaka wood, to which has been added many new buildings to meet the hi-tech agricultural output of this island. Tourists as such do not visit this hardworking, functional island, although the island has both an airstrip and boat landing stage.

ALDABRA

Aldabra, believed to be the world's largest atoll and largest sea lagoon, is made up of a rugged ring of coral tufted with thick scrub. It sits atop a volcanic base and is surrounded by turbulent reef that rapidly disappears as if down a mountain slope into the depths of the sea. 34km (21 miles) long, and 14.5km (9 miles) across, the land area of the 14 islands around the ring of atoll is only slightly less than that of Mahé, although its lagoon alone could almost swallow the mountainous main island. It lies 1200km (750 miles) from the granitic islands, and about half that from mainland Africa, a distant, unique sanctuary for ancient animal, flora, and marine life.

The shallow green **lagoon** is dotted with umbrellas of coral that emerge like mushrooms at low tide to provide landing pads for legions of daft booby birds and frigates. The whole lagoon, lined with barriers of mangrove, empties in a tidal rush every 12 hours through three main passes. At these times it is impossible to make headway in a boat against the turbulence. Yet, in the evening or early morning, and particularly when one of Aldabra's sudden squalls builds up across the lagoon, the shallow water can be a panorama of pastel colours quickly softening the mirror of heat from sea and sky.

Aldabra, rising an unusually high (for a coral island) 8m (26ft) above the naviga-

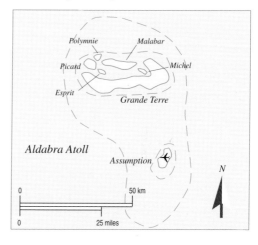

Aldabra Atoll

tor's horizon, was named by Arab seamen over 1000 years ago. Aldabra could be a version of 'al-khadra', Arabic for green, as it must have seemed startlingly colourful after Arabia, but it could also refer to the heavenly constellation, Aldebaran. In 1964, Aldabra was nearly raised to build a joint British-US airbase. Conservationists worldwide, alerted by Seychellois leaders, raised the alarm and Aldabra's rare wonderland was saved. Since 1967 it has been a major scientific research centre.

GETTING TO ALDABRA

The nearest airstrip is on Assumption, a three-hour boat ride away. Even then Assumption is normally beyond the range of the Air Seychelles domestic fleet, and only special flights will land there. There are only a dozen or so people living on Aldabra, and there are no visitor facilities. Special permission is needed to visit the island – it is rarely given, but can be obtained from: The Seychelles Island Foundation, c/o Ministry of Tourism, P.O. Box 92, Victoria, Mahé, Seychelles; fax: (248) 225131.

Flora

Aldabra is no verdant honeymoon isle of silvery sands and whispering palms. Covered in ragged **pemphis scrub,** with the occasional line of **casuarinas** and twisted **palms**, the weather-ravaged surface of the steel grey-coloured coral is like walking across a moonscape of ferociously pitted molten limestone. At the edge of the lagoon the undercut cliffs hang over the water, and when the southeast trades blow, whipping up the water, spray blows up through the holes like angry geysers. Despite the semi-arid, desolate feel, however, the atoll boasts 273 species of flowering shrub and fern, 19 of which grow only on Aldabra and another 22 on only one other island.

Apart from the Aldabra **screw pines** (or *bwa d'amande*) and huge stands of mangroves that line the lagoon, a number of species advertise their rarity with the prefix Aldabra in their name. Two of these, as if cocking a snoot at their harsh environment with sweet fragrances and delicate flowers, are **Aldabra jasmine** and the **Aldabra lily**. The two areas on Aldabra where the landscape is a little more gentle are along the fringes fertilized by seabird guano where gnarled **mapou trees** grow, and among the sand dunes in the south.

Below: *Tortoises flourishing, if not hurrying, on their remote and protected home of Aldabra.*

Fauna

Birds, of course, are born to fly. The few flightless species around the world tend to be quite well known, with the solitaire of Rodrigues and the dodo of Mauritius perhaps the best known of them all. In the Indian Ocean, however, all are dead and gone, except for Aldabra's **white-throated rail**, the little olive green and rather tame bird that pecks about

the bush. Rare, though rather unspectacular to look at, the rail is joined by the unique **Aldabra drongo** with its forked tail, and the skulking **Aldabra warbler**.

In addition there are thousands of other **terns**, **tropic birds** and **boobies** rising from the mangroves. The boobies are known as *fou* (daft) in Kreol, possibly because they are easily frightened into disgorging their catch by bullying **frigate birds** who breed in tens of thousands on

Above: *The drainage channels at the western end of Aldabra's lagoon.*
Below: *A large bat fish, known as* poulet d'eau, *and a scuba diver.*

THE ALDABRA GOATS

Among the incredible and unusual wildlife on Aldabra, the last thing you would expect to find is a plain old goat. The Aldabra goats are a throwback to the days when the British Navy would drop off a couple of the hardy animals, and perhaps plant a few coconut trees, on remote islands and atolls so that shipwreck victims had some hope of survival when they drifted onto the inevitable desert island.

Above: *One of Aldabra's pitted, mushroom-shaped coral formations, popular nesting platforms for birds.*

DINOSAURS

Although they can swim quite well, it is unlikely that the Aldabran tortoise came to the atoll from the Galapagos, halfway around the world and the only other natural habitat of giant tortoises. On land, they can manage 30m (100ft) an hour, but the unstressed attitude pays off, as they can also go for weeks without food, and have been reported to live for 150 years. The tortoise goes back to dinosaur days, a species even older than the Nile crocodiles that used to terrify early Seychellois settlers.

Aldabra. **Flamingoes** can be seen, as well as the striking **Aldabra sacred ibis**, while the **Aldabra souimanga sunbirds** are far more colourful than their granitic island cousins. The **Aldabra fruit bat,** with its distinctive white face, cruises in the evening between the trees.

Possibly the strangest of all creatures on this living museum is the large **robber** or **coconut crab**. This reddish-pink, sometimes green monster, a land-breathing crab which can grow up to 60cm (2ft) long, likes to hide away under rocks and skuttle up coconut trees at night to rip open the green nuts with its huge pincers.

The Aldabra Group

Cosmoledo atoll, Astove, and Assumption Island are part of the Aldabra group. **Cosmoledo** is a 19km (12 mile) atoll broken up into 12 islands, whose reefs are littered with wrecks. Sailing close to the ring of islands can be hazardous as its landfalls (with names such as Wizard, Mosquito and Pagoda) are widely separated but linked by silent but deadly reef. The harvesting of turtle, guano and green snail (taken for mother of pearl) denuded Cosmoledo of much of its flora and fauna, although the atoll is still very attractive. It is a source of sooty tern eggs, though only a few workers inhabit this lonely atoll.

Astove, to the south of Cosmoledo, was another of the pirates' haunts. It is an almost perfect ring atoll with just one break into its lovely, beach-lined 5km (3 mile) long lagoon. The inhabitants of the island export copra, salted fish, and reed brooms to distant Mahé.

Assumption, to the west of Cosmoledo, and 30km (19 miles) south of Aldabra, is the staging post for Aldabra, with a newly constructed airstrip, and accommodation available. Once another great source of guano, these days its sand is highly valued by the construction industry on the Inner Islands.

FARQUHAR GROUP

Farquhar can occasionally be lashed with terrible cyclones that sneak across the Indian Ocean from the northwest during the months of January and February. Winds of up to 120 knots ('just beginning to turn me on' as Seychelles yachtsman Brownie will tell you at Victoria's Yacht Club) howl across the two largest islands and their great circlet of reef, whipping the palms and cutting a swathe of destruction like a scythe across the islands. Underwater the terrible convulsions of the ocean heave and crash the corals as if in an avalanche.

Amirantes Group   *Mahé*

Alphonse Group

Aldabra Group   I N D I A N
O C E A N

Farquhar Group

CORAL ATOLLS

One of Charles Darwin's aims during his circumnavigation on the *Beagle* was to determine the formation of coral atolls. His view (which is still widely recognised) is that atolls are the final stage of a continuing upgrowth of coral around a sinking volcanic island. Coral is also always growing outwards from the centre of an atoll, favouring the ocean-facing side where plankton is richer than in the water of the lagoon.

Below: *A cloud betrays Assumption melting into the horizon.*

FRIGATE BIRDS

- Known as the pirates of the air, they live by harrying other sea birds and forcing them to disgorge or drop their fish.
- There are five species in the world, two of which have important colonies on Aldabra atoll.
- They are jet black, angular, almost stylised birds, with long wings and a distinctive forked tail.
- The male frigate bird has a red patch under its chin which it will inflate to impress its mate.

Below: *Tenuous tranquility on Farquhar, Seychelles' cyclone territory.*

No wonder that Farquhar, discovered in 1504 by João de Nova, the Portuguese navigator, and its neighbour Providence, have the deadliest shipwreck record in Seychelles, some 12 in all. In this century alone, Providence has been responsible for the loss of the *Jorgen Bank*, the *Endeavour*, *S.S. Syria* and at least one schooner, the *Maggie Low*.

Make it past the treacherous reefs and strong currents of the narrow pass into the Farquhar lagoon, and it is one of the safest and loveliest anchorages in the islands. Farquhar is lush with palms and casuarinas growing down to white beaches. There is a settlement there, a phone, and a seldom-used airstrip. The islands are 710km (440 miles) from Mahé, which is usually beyond the range of the Air Seychelles air fleet.

The group takes its name from Sir Robert Farquhar, a governor of Mauritius, and in fact these islands were only transferred from Mauritius to Seychelles in 1921. Only Providence and Farquhar are inhabited.

Pattern of Islands at a Glance

Best Times to Visit

The granitic islands in particular have heavy rains starting in **October** and lasting until **April**. The coral islands receive less rain but it can be erratic with sudden, heavy showers any time of year. It is less humid on the Coral islands and there is usually a sea breeze. Being flat and often exposed, the temperatures are a little higher. Farquhar atoll can suffer cyclones, particularly between December and February.

Getting There

Most of the islands have no regular air or sea service, and transport to and from the islands tends to be organized by the resorts themselves.
Bird. Daily half-hour flight, booked with accommodation.
Denis. Flights four times a week. Also helicopter. Again booked with accommodation.
Silhouette. Helicopter, tel: 375400, or launch from Marine Charter, tel: 322126.
North Island. Contact Marine Charter, tel: 322126.
Frégate. Helicopter, airflight, or luxury launch. Booked with accommodation.
Amirantes. There are flights accompanying lodge bookings for Desroches. Otherwise it is 24 hours by yacht: contact Marine Charter. Chartered flights can be arranged to D'Arros and other islands.
Plate. Schooner or motor launch; contact Marine Charter, tel: 322126.

Coétivy. Has an airstrip, but charter flights only, or yacht.
Aldabra. By air to Assumption and then yacht. Astove island also has an airstrip but not Cosmoledo.
Farquhar group. Has airstrip but possibly too far for small Mahé-based aircraft.

For permission to visit Aldabra, contact Seychelles Islands Foundation, Box 92, Mahé, fax: 225131. For Cosmoledo, Farquhar and the other distant islands: Island Development Co., Box 638, Mahé, fax: 224467.

Getting Around

There are very few roads on the smaller granitic and coraline islands. There is the occasional **bicycle** but the normal means of transport is to **walk**. Longer trips to the far side of the larger islands would be done by small **boats** with an outboard engine.

Where to Stay

Lodges or resorts are often the only ones on a particular island; generally they are small, luxurious, and exclusive.
Bird Island Lodge. Newly-built, roomy bungalows. Seychellois-English run; tel: 224925, fax: 225074.
Denis Island Lodge. Luxury under thatch. French owners; tel: 321143, fax: 321010.
Silhouette Lodge. Chalets and palms. Italian run; tel: 229003, fax: 344178.
Frégate Lodge. Wooden plantation-style chalets among flowering trees; tel: 323123, fax: 324169.
Desroches Island Lodge. Away from it all. Lovely chalets and pristine beach; tel: 229003, fax: 344178. Many of the other islands have private rudimentary plantation houses or shacks, but as the only way to get to the island is by yacht, it makes more sense to stay on board.

Where to Eat

All those islands with lodges have excellent kitchens. Other than boutiques in these lodges, there are no shops except those providing bare essentials to the workers on each island.

Activities and Excursions

Day trips by helicopter or boat, and occasionally by aircraft, are possible to some of the islands. Contact any tour operator (below) to make arrangements. Fishing, sailing, diving, snorkelling, nature walks are usually offered at all the islands with lodges.

Useful telephone Numbers

Air Seychelles, tel: 225220. Helicopter Seychelles, tel: 375400.
Tour operators: Mason's, tel: 322642; Bunson Travel (Tailor-made specialist excursions), tel: 322682; TSS, tel: 322414; NTS, tel: 224900.
Seychelles Islands Foundation, tel: 225313 (Ask for Mr Lindsay Chung-Seng.)

Travel Tips

Tourist Information

Seychelles maintains Tourist Offices in the following cities around the world:

France (Paris),
tel: 428 98685
Germany (Frankfurt),
tel: (069) 292064
Italy (Milan),
tel: (02) 4985795
Japan (Tokyo),
tel: (03) 562342
Hong Kong,
tel: 86526552
Kenya (Nairobi),
tel: (02) 25103
Sweden (Stockholm),
tel: 240716
Singapore,
tel: 2557373
South Africa (Johannesburg),
c/o Air Seychelles,
tel: (011) 4873556
Spain, c/o Air Marketing,
tel: 3195189
United Kingdom (London),
tel: (071) 2241670
USA (New York),
tel: (212) 6879766.

In Seychelles:
Department of Tourism and Transport, Seychelles, P.O. Box 92, Mahé, tel: (248) 225313, fax: (248) 224035.

The main **Tourist Information Office,** tel: 225313, is in Victoria, on the ground floor of Independence House, which is on the right hand side of Independence Avenue, about 200m from the Clock Tower travelling towards the harbour. There is also an office at the Airport, tel: 373136, and hotels are always a good source of information.

Entry Requirements

A valid passport is required but Seychelles does not require visas. All visitors are automatically given a one month pass which can be extended for a small fee provided you have a return ticket and sufficient funds. (For further details contact Department of Internal Affairs, Immigration Division, Independence House, Victoria, tel: 225333).

Health Requirements

Nil. Seychelles is free of such common tropical diseases as malaria, typhoid, dysentery and bilharzia.

Customs

Firearms, underwater spearguns, animals, drugs (other than personal medicinal), and agricultural and horticultural products are all banned. 200 cigarettes and 1.5 litres of any alcoholic drink are duty free. Even if you go through the green route there will probably be a cursory examination of your luggage. There is a 15 year jail sentence for cannabis smuggling and special permission is required to export a coco de mer.

Travel to Seychelles

Mahé is the only port of entry for **international flights**. The airport is on the eastern side of the island at Pointe La Rue, about 15 minutes drive from the centre of Victoria. Aircraft and helicopter services are available from there to many of the smaller islands. Air Seychelles uses the latest aircraft and flies from London, Johannesburg, Nairobi and a variety of European, Middle and Far Eastern capitals.

Consult your travel agent for details of **cruise ships** calling at Seychelles. If you are arriving by **yacht**, contact the Department of Tourism beforehand, especially if you are anchoring at islands other than Mahé, tel: (248) 225313, fax: (248) 225131/ 224035 for appropriate permissions. Or contact Port Victoria Harbour Control, tel: 224701 (24 hours).

There is no departure tax other than that included in your ticket.

Travel in Seychelles

On Mahé and perhaps Praslin you will want to hire a **car**. Cars drive on the left, there is a minimum age limit of 21, and you will need your valid national or international driving licence. The speed limit is 65kph (40mph in Victoria). There are no traffic lights in Seychelles. **Maps:** *Globetrotter Travel Map* of Seychelles provides detailed information; other maps are available from the Survey Office, Victoria.

Taxis are relatively expensive, but the cars are sound and the drivers good. Check fares first if there is no meter. Call: Victoria, tel: 323739/ 322279; Beau Vallon, tel: 247499; Airport, tel: 373349/ 373119; Barbarons, tel: 378629; Praslin airport, tel: 233429; Praslin schooner jetty, tel: 233859.

There are good **bus** services on Mahé and Praslin. They are painted white. You will see the bus stop signs on the tarmac roads. The main terminus in Victoria is on the corner of Palm Street and 5th June Avenue. The service seldom

extends beyond 19:00 on Mahé, or 17:30 on Praslin. **Bicycles** are available for hire on Mahé, Praslin and La Digue. **Both yachts** and **big game fishing boats** can be chartered from Marine Charter in Victoria. The inter-island **ferries** are large motor-sailing schooners, and operate between Mahé, Praslin and La Digue, as do luxury motor cruisers from Marine Charter. Air Seychelles operates regular **inter-island flights**, particularly between Mahé and Praslin, Bird, Denis, Frégate, and Desroches islands, tel: 225220.

Clothes: What to Pack

Light tropical clothing. Possibly a light jacket or sweater, though you are unlikely to need it. Bring swimming costume, broad brimmed hat, umbrella, sun barrier, dark glasses and sandals. A pair of long trousers is needed for the evening. Also useful are a torch for after dark, binoculars for bird watching and lots of camera film. Snorkelling equipment is always worth having.

Money Matters

There are no exchange control regulations other than a maximum export of 100 Rupees (Rs) in Seychelles currency. The Seychelles **rupee**, which is divided into 100 cents, comes in note denominations of Rs100, Rs50, Rs25 and Rs10. There are approximately Rs7.50 to the British pound. Hotels and most shops accept credit cards, travel cheques

and cash. There are **banks** on the main islands; they are only open in the mornings: 08:30 to 13:00 Monday to Friday. Some banks are also open on Saturday and Barclays (Albert St Branch) opens in the afternoons 14:00 to 16:00 for travellers cheque transactions. Airport banks are open for flights only. Do not leave it until the last minute to cash in your rupees as the banks do not always have the foreign currency you require. The bank on La Digue opens Tuesday and Thursday 10:30 to 14:00 only.

Tipping at about 10% is not compulsory, but for good service it is appropriate. Check to see if service has been included in your bill.

Accommodation

Seychelles has a number of **large hotels**, usually on the best beaches on Mahé and Praslin. They have swimming pools, tennis courts and many other amenities, and are ideal if you are on a package holiday. There are smaller, more exclusive, and quite costly hotels on Mahé, Praslin and La Digue, most of which have excellent restaurants. There are also a large number of **guest houses** which are the best way to pick up the flavour of the islands. Many people book into one of these for three nights and then look around. The outer coral islands have magnificent coral island beaches and Bird Island, Silhouette, Desroches and others have exclusive **luxury lodges**.

The government has set a limit of 4500 hotel beds in Seychelles, a number which is unlikely to be increased substantially in the near future. There are **no camping facilities** anywhere on the islands, and generally visitors have to book their accommodation before they arrive.

Nearly all hotels and guest houses serve excellent meals, and there is a wide selection of **restaurants** mainly concentrating on Kreol and French cuisine. Seafood dishes predominate.

Trading Hours

Shops and businesses are closed on Saturday afternoons and Sundays, although some rural shops open at odd hours over the weekend and late in the evenings. Normal business hours are 08:00 to 16:00, with a one hour break 12:00 to 13:00 when some will shut. Many shops do not open until 09:00, but make up for it by closing at 17:00. Note that the banks all close at 13:00.

Measurements

Seychelles uses the metric system throughout.

Communications

Cable and Wireless have provided Seychelles with a superb **telephone**, **telex** and **fax** system. There are pay phones everywhere (usually using cards which can be purchased at Cable and Wireless, post offices, and other general outlets). The Seychelles telephone directory is a colourful mine of information. There is a local **TV and radio** station and some hotels offer CNN via satellite dishes. There are convenient **post offices** on the major granitic islands. Seychelles stamps are colourful and often treasured by collectors. There is a philatelic bureau at the main post office near the clock tower in Victoria, tel: 225222.

The international code for phoning Seychelles is 248.
Operator, tel: 100
International operator, tel: 151
Directory Enquiries, tel: 181
Emergencies, tel: 999.
Seychelles time is GMT + 4.

Electricity

240 AC; plugs are 3-pin (square). Remember to bring a torch as there aren't always street lights, particularly in rural areas of Mahé and on the smaller islands.

Medical Services

There is an excellent **hospital** at Mount Fleuri, near the Botanical Gardens, with x-ray, pathology, and all facilities, tel: 224400.

Dental services are also available, tel: 224400.
There are **small hospitals or clinics** at many of the little villages on Mahé, Praslin, and La Digue.
Private medical doctors:
Dr Maurice Albert, tel: 323866; Dr K.S. Chetty, tel: 371911.
Pharmacies:
Foch Heng, tel: 322751 (after hours, tel: 241233); Behram's, tel: 225559; George Lilams, tel: 321733.
The hospital dispensary opens Monday-Friday 08:00 to 18:00, and Saturdays 08:30 to 12:30.
Optometrists, tel: 321993 or 321177.

Emergencies

Ambulance, Police, Fire, tel: 999
Hospital, Mount Fleuri, Mahé, tel: 224400

Health Hazards

The **tap water** is perfectly safe and bottled water is available. There is no malaria or bilharzia in Seychelles. Milk is pasteurised and usually long life. Air conditioning

CONVERSION CHART		
FROM	**TO**	**MULTIPLY BY**
Millimetres	Inches	0.0394
Metres	Yards	1.0936
Metres	Feet	3.281
Kilometres	Miles	0.6214
Hectares	Acres	2.471
Litres	Pints	1.760
Kilograms	Pounds	2.205
Tonnes	Tons	0.984
To convert Celsius to Fahrenheit: x 9 ÷ 5 + 32		

sometimes leads to colds and flu as you acclimatise. Seychelles are just south of the equator so the **sun** is hot and should be diligently protected against.

Avoid the rare **centipede** and **scorpion.** The four species of **snake,** which are usually only seen in the high forests, are non-poisonous, but can bite. Apart from the sun, the most commonly encountered hazards are around the sea. Beaches with seaweed lying heavy on them tend to have scratchy **sandflies. Coral scratches** are normally not dangerous in themselves, but treat them immediately as they quickly become infected. Wear shoes when walking on exposed reef or in seaweedy or grey sand water, but watch where you walk. **Sea urchin spines** should be removed if they come out easily, but left if they don't. As with **jellyfish stings,** immerse the infected area in the hottest water you can stand, which will help inactivate the toxin, and then seek further medical advice. Avoid touching cone shells. The ugly **stonefish** that lurks in sand underwater is deadly but rarely encountered. **Aids,** as everywhere, is found in Seychelles.

Security

Seychelles is a fairly wealthy country with practically no beggars. Bag snatching is almost unheard of and petty theft is not common, though locking your car is always a good precaution. The country is well policed, with stations

usually in every village. Central Police Station, Victoria, tel: 322011. Violent crime is rare. Women are safe in Seychelles; it is a largely matriarchal society. Still, avoid obvious risks such as walking about alone at night or swimming at a deserted beach.

PUBLIC HOLIDAYS

January 1st and 2nd New year public holiday
Good Friday
Easter Sunday
Labour Day 1 May
Liberation Day 5 June
National Day 18 June
Independence Day 29 June
Assumption Day (La Digue Festival) 15 August
All Saints' Day 1 November
Feast of the Immaculate Conception 8 December
Christmas Day 25 December

Language

Kreol, a language mainly derived from French (but written phonetically and therefore difficult to decipher at first from its French origins) is the official language. English is normally used in the shops and French is widely understood. Some road signs are also in Italian and German, languages understood by many tour operators and hoteliers.

Sports

The following are available:
Golf. Reef Golf Club Hotel, tel: 376251.

Tennis and Squash. Many hotels. Try Equator Sun, Reef, Le Meridien Barbarons; also National Sports Council courts in Mont Fleuri, tel: 224770.
Windsurfing. Try Beau Vallon Bay, Mahé Beach Hotel, and Côte d'Or, Praslin.
Riding. Le Meridien Barbarons, tel: 378253; also on La Digue.
Sailing. The Yacht Club in Victoria welcomes temporary members, tel: 322362. Enquire there or at neighbouring Marine Charter for details on chartering boats.
Diving (and learning to dive). Underwater Centre, Coral Strand Hotel, tel: 247357. Also Marine Divers at Le Northolme Hotel, tel: 261222, Beau Vallon Bay Hotel, tel: 247141, and on Praslin, La Digue, Silhouette, and Desroches islands.
Deep-sea fishing. Marine Charter, tel: 322126.
Waterskiing. Various hotels and operators at Beau Vallon Bay and elsewhere.
Surfing. Sometimes at Grand'Anse in Mahé. Not many boards in Seychelles.
Paragliding. Beau Vallon Bay. Beach operators.
Walking. There are a number of marked trails on Mahé. Leaflet guides are available from the Tourist Information Office in Victoria.

Nightlife

Most large hotels offer folk-dancing , fish barbecues, and dinner-dances. Nightclubs in Victoria include the Love Nut. There is also a cinema, discos, and amateur theatre.

INDEX